Japanese Cherry Blossoms symbolize ne'
each precious moment. In Japanese trac
these blossoms only live for a short perioc
opportunities and a revival of the soul. I chose cherry blossoms for the covei
of this book because their spiritual message brings forth the opportunity for
transformation. I believe all of us have the opportunity to live more
abundant and joyful lives as we become more mindful and aware of our
choices. The cherry blossom reminds us to value what is important, to
acknowledge our own magnificence, to live in the moment, and to always
give gratitude for what we have.

Sherri Divband is the owner of Intuitive Wellness, a Center for
Spiritual and Holistic Healing in Bethesda Maryland. If you would like
more information about Intuitive Wellness please visit
IntuitiveWellnessCenter.com

I would like to thank

My husband and best friend Kas for his continued support throughout our journey together. You have been by my side throughout the best and most difficult times. You are my number one fan, my rock, and you ground me when I need it most. I love you more and more each day.

My children, Jordan, Skyler and Aramis, for opening up my heart in ways I never knew possible. I have grown, I have broken down, and I have blossomed. Through it all, l have all of you to thank for that. You take me out of my comfort zone, you hold me accountable, and most importantly your love is expansive and powerful. Even in the most difficult times, a hug from you will heal all my wounds. You bring light and joy into my life. My love for you is endless.

My mother, Pamela, for encouraging me to move forward even during the times I wanted to quit. When I didn't believe in myself, you did. You are always available when I need you. Your support has been unconditional. My love and respect for you goes far beyond this time and space.

My mother-in-law, Simin, for your willingness to help us in any way you can. You provide a second home for our children, and we will always cherish your love and support.

My father, Bill, for your continued love and support. I am always grateful for your guidance, and I cherish our time together.

My friend, Charles, for donating his time to editing this book. There is no other person I would have trusted to take my vision and turn it into an organized, legible, and incredible book. I am honored to have you as family and a dear friend.

My dear friend Jenny, for giving feedback and edits on the original manuscript. I have so much gratitude for your kindness.

All of my closest friends for supporting me throughout this journey, I am grateful for each and every one of you.

Intuitive Transformation Evolution

First Edition 2019

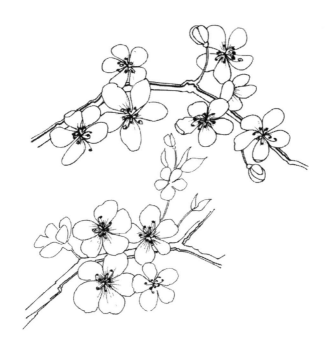

Intuitive Transformation Evolution

Table of Contents

Author's Forward - Intuitive Transformation Evolution Process

Section 1: Intuition

Section 2: Transformation

Intuitive Transformation Evolution Process

Intuitive Transformation Evolution (ITE) is a self-healing process I created to enable people to take back their power, identify what is causing blockages in their life, and enable them to release negative emotions. These combined elements would work, in concert, to bring them peace and balance. We have evolved to a time where our bodies give us the signs needed to make the lifestyle changes required to truly heal. A vast majority of us rely heavily on our healthcare system and pharmaceuticals to dictate our health and, therefore, our well-being. In turn, our power is being taken from us, and we are left being disconnected with what our bodies really need in order to thrive. As a society, we have lost our connection to Mother Earth and nature. We operate in survival mode by competing with those around us instead of combining resources to lift each other up. Our society has become brainwashed with what the media portrays as *normal* and *accepted.* If we do not live up to those expectations, we feel as though we have failed in some way.

This uniform way of living has caused high levels of stress and loss of balance. Many people are living in a way where they are completely disconnected from themselves. We have lost our true essence, who we are as individuals and who we strive to be - - not because of what society expects of us, but what we truly desire. This causes disharmony within our body because, on some level, our body recognizes the internal struggle between *what you do* and *who you are.* We may be able to put on a facade for those around us that we are happy. Whether we do it to please others, or to prove to ourselves we can be molded into a preferred way, our bodies know the truth. Our bodies hold, not only the energy and the thoughts that we put out in the universe, but also the emotions we keep inside. If you are not operating from a place of truth, your body will not be in balance. It is our emotions and our thoughts that dictate our health and our well-being.

Since words, thoughts and emotions carry energy, they vibrate differently depending on whether the emotion is heavy or light. For instance, if you are in a state of anger or fear, your energetic vibration will be low and dense; the energy flow in and out of the body will become disrupted and unbalanced, making you feel fatigued and not yourself. Whereas, if you are happy and vibrant, your vibrational frequency will elevate, making you feel euphoric, as the energy flow throughout the body is functioning efficiently. When we are in a state of constant worry and anxiety, the energy flow throughout our body is disrupted and may cease to flow all together. When the energy distribution is not flowing efficiently, our immune system and other vital functions in our body operate at a life-sustaining level as opposed to an optimal level.

If our autonomic nervous system is operating in sympathetic mode a majority of the time due to chronic stress, also known as *fight-or-flight*, this puts our body in survival mode. Because our bodies are pretty amazing, they eventually adapt to the environment to increase the likelihood of survival. The bad news is that our bodies can't operate in that mode for too long. Our bodies give us signs to let us know that we need to slow down. At first they may be subtle, such as tension headaches, rashes or minor colds. However, if we don't listen, the symptoms become more severe. Because we live in a time where we tend to treat the symptom and not the cause, we are prescribed medicine to make the symptoms go away. This is only a temporary fix, and the symptoms will undoubtedly come back if we don't resolve the underlying issue. Then we have side effects from the medication prescribed, and we are given another drug to treat those side-effects, which in turn causes another set of issues. Suddenly, we find ourselves headed down a path of chasing symptoms. Instead of feeling better, we are left frustrated and confused. We need to break this cycle and tap into our innate ability to transform our bodies into a more balanced homeostatic state.

Throughout my journey as an Intuitive Healer, I have seen more people in the past few years who are fed up with the way they are living, and seek the answers to how they can break free from this cycle. It is so encouraging to see an abundance of people who are finally ready to take back their power and to truly embrace their ability to use their own intuition to initiate their own healing process. To understand how I can enable people to take the driver's seat in their healing journey, I must first explain how my sessions have evolved.

When I first started my energy sessions, I was excited because I combined all of my certifications, trainings, and the knowledge I had gained on all facets of the healing modalities I was interested in. I developed my own unique way to navigate my sessions, and customized them based on what the individual needed at the time, whether that was pain management, accelerated healing after surgeries, stress management, trauma release or general balance and wellness. I was really helping people, and I was making a difference in, not only their health and wellness, but their awareness. Over time, I began giving Intuitive guidance in my sessions. However, for a period of time, I was unsure if people would be open to receiving guidance in that way, so I kept that part to myself. I always received images and guidance during my sessions from the person's guides or angels, or even their higher self. In the early stages of my work, I was insecure and worried that, if I divulged these messages to people, they would run for the hills never to be seen again. I allowed my own insecurities to hinder my ability to help people in a more well-rounded way. You see, the Intuitive guidance that I received for people often explained why they were experiencing that particular symptom, and how they were holding themselves back. I could see how their emotions drove their mind, which caused their body to react accordingly. Instead of explaining the cycle to them, I simply did the energy session, re-balanced their chakras, lessened their inflammation and pain, and stopped there. I started having more and more people come to me who were spiritual and open based on how they spoke to me, and the things they said. So, I started to give small amounts of information to these people after the session to see how they would react. If it was positive, I would give them more. I was training myself with positive reinforcement, much like you would do with a puppy--- I was a registered Veterinary Technician also working at the National Zoo at the time, so it seemed only fitting. To my surprise and slight apprehension, I suddenly became known as the energy healer who gave Intuitive guidance in her sessions. I went from being insecure, to excited at the openness of others, back to insecure again. Because this guidance was now suddenly expected, I became worried about whether I would lose the ability, or even worse, give the wrong guidance.

I decided to let the fear go, as I was all too aware of how fear lowers your vibrational state. I knew I had to replace that emotion with a combination of excitement and also the release of expectation, as I could not forget why I was doing the energy sessions to begin with. I wanted to help others balance their energy and emotions, to bring them clarity, better health, and a better life. The Intuitive guidance had to be second to the goal of their overall wellness. Once I released that burden, to my surprise, my connection with the Divine became stronger, as did my Intuition. I suddenly found myself transforming people's lives by helping them discover the source of their energetic and emotional blockages, and empowering them to heal on their own. In this way, they wouldn't need me to be in the driver's seat of their healing journey. I would become simply a passenger and a mentor to guide them on their way. This process became incredibly empowering for both me and those that came to see me. I was discovering ways to enhance and to bring forth our innate ability to call upon our own inner power, to release trapped emotions, and to develop a new sense of self that stemmed from a place of balance, reflection and realignment of the mind, body and soul.

Throughout my own healing journey of motherhood, wife, business owner, entrepreneur, energy healer, and life coach, I have found my own struggles to remain balanced. It is throughout my journey of helping others while also helping myself, that I discovered the Intuitive Transformation Evolution. This is a process that has taken years to manifest, through personal evolution, making mistakes, left turns and right turns, roadblocks and golden passageways, succeeding and failing -- all bringing me to where I am today. I offer this process of directing your own healing journey through your Intuition, your ability to transform into anything you want to be, and to evolve by elevating yourself, and, in turn, elevating the world around you. I believe we are headed in that direction, and each and every person can make a difference. They can play their part in elevating the planet, if not for themselves, then for their children and their children's children who deserve more than we are giving in our current world. It is about evolving, turning towards each other - not turning away, reflecting inward, and not judging others. It's about spreading love and compassion to as many people as we can. It is about healing Mother Earth, and healing ourselves first before we can truly help others. It is about thriving as a community, not just as an individual, and building bridges to bring us together, not walls to separate us. I invite you to begin your Spiritual awakening by following the Intuitive Transformation Evolution - a process of self-discovery, release, realignment, redirecting, and rejoicing.

Intuitive Transformation Evolution is a simple three-step process which involves a commitment to healing the mind, body, and soul through self-reflection, recognizing triggers, and releasing unwanted emotions using your Intuition as a guide. By rediscovering yourself through a transformational process of unraveling the parts of yourself that have stemmed from a life of pre-programming, like an onion, you will peel back the layers of yourself that are no longer needed. Through visualization and Intention, you will step on a new path - one of clarity, empowerment and strength. With this newly found freedom, you will then be ready to evolve into the bestversion of yourself, where the possibilities are endless.

Section 1: Intuition

"Out beyond the ideas of wrongdoing and rightdoing there is a field. I'll meet you there"
-Rumi

Chapter One
What is Intuition?

Your Intuition is the part of yourself that you have the ability to tap into whenever you need, to help guide you to make the choices that are truly best for your well-being. To begin, it is important to understand the difference between following your Intuition and listening to your conscious mind or the inner voice in your head. Think of your conscious mind as the engine and your body as the vehicle. Your Intuition is the electrical system that controls every aspect of its performance. You need the engine to keep things moving, to respond quickly to the changes in the road ahead, to withstand extreme heat and cold, and to drive bumpy roads and smooth ones. Your conscious mind keeps things moving along by guiding you on what you should do moment-to-moment in your life - in real time. Your conscious mind is the voice in your head telling you what to do and what not to do.

Unfortunately, our conscious mind is surface level, and it is the part of *you* that can give the worst advice because it is susceptible to your emotional state. If you are in a positive mindset, it can tell you that you can do anything, that you can reach for the stars and touch them. However, if you are in a state of fear, and your vibration is low due to that fear, that same voice can convince you that you will fail at just about anything. Our inner voice can be our greatest asset, and also our worst nemesis. I am sure you have encountered the inner conflict at many points in your life, when you were forced to make a choice, to go one direction or the other. Whether that choice was about school, a job, or a relationship, you needed to choose one route or another, and your inner voice likely played many roles. These roles were those parts of yourself that wanted to go one way or another, much like a play performing internally in your mind, and you weighed out each option, visualizing how it would play out. Your inner voice would weigh-in by persuading you one way or the other, and I am sure there were times that your inner voice would caution against what you had chosen to do, leaving you lost, trying to figure out which voice to listen to. Our conscious mind can allow us to open the door to the vast potential of possibilities, but that can backfire should we allow it to control us. We often listen to our conscious mind for the wrong reasons, whether it be self-doubt, anxiety or lack of self-worth, and we end up caving, and going the wrong direction. What we need to do in those moments is follow our Intuition --- and quiet the part of our self which makes us choose based on the wrong emotional mindset.

Your Intuition is important. It is that electrical system in your vehicle, complex and magnificent because it has an important job to do. Your intuition taps into your subconscious, the part of you that stores the memories of not only this life, but all of your lives. It holds the answers to just about anything you want to know because it gives you information based on the whole picture, not just parts of it. Your subconscious, also known as your Higher Self, is always looking out for what is best for you, and, if you learn to trust in it, it will never let you down. The important thing is discerning and understanding the difference between the conscious mind, or the Ego, and the subconscious. For the purposes of making it simple to understand, let's assign the conscious mind the role of the *Nemesis* and the subconscious mind the role of the *Friend*. One of the easiest ways to know if you are being guided by your *Friend*, is to be mindful of your emotional state. If you are in a place of worry, anger, stress, sadness, fear, resentment, or even extreme fatigue, your *Nemesis* will try and swoop in and lead you in a direction best suited for *its* own agenda. Your *Nemesis* is not always looking out for what is best for you, but what is the easiest route to take. Your *Friend* would encourage you to relax, take a deep breath, and take a moment before making any decisions. Because we often are quick to make decisions from an emotional state, we are operating from a lower vibration. This means the energy around us is dense and heavy, which is not a recipe for good decision making. When your vibration is low, that means that the energy around you is also low, and it is extremely difficult to receive guidance from your *Friend*. Imagine your *Friend* is in another state, and she is trying to give you advice over the phone. If the connection is bad, you can barely hear anything she is trying to say, and the call can drop, and you can't even speak to her at all. This is what happens when you are in a lower emotional mindset, you become trapped there, and the only one that can get to you in that space is your *Nemesis*. No matter how hard you try to reach your *Friend*, the line is busy.

This is the reason that many of us make poor choices which we regret later; because we received guidance from the wrong part of our self, we were taken advantage of in our moment of weakness. Think about all of the times that you regretted your decision the next day, when you were clearer headed, you had a night's sleep, or you were not crying anymore; you had calmed down and suddenly had a different perspective. When we are in a more balanced mindset, our vibration is much higher, giving us unlimited access to our *Friend*, whenever we need her.

How do we talk to our Friend?

In order to have a clearer connection with our *Friend*, our subconscious, we need to develop a good rapport, so that we learn to trust the guidance we receive. Some of us have become so dependent on our *Nemesis*, that we have actually become "friendly." As a result, we take our *Nemesis'* advice as truth --- much like an unhealthy relationship, we become addicted, complacent and accepting of our *Nemesis'* unhealthy judgement. In order to develop a good relationship with your true *Friend*, you must learn how to evict your *Nemesis*. This process starts with finding balance, a concept that may feel foreign to you. However, I can assure you that if you follow the ITE steps, you will not only evict your *Nemesis*, you and your *Friend* will become equal partners in your healing journey.

When you begin to engage with your Higher Self, take notice of your emotional state which will directly affect your connection. Meditation is one of the best ways to quiet the conscious mind, which also happens to be the most challenging part of meditation. Most people are unable to quiet their mind when they attempt to meditate, which causes distraction and frustration. Furthermore, it becomes even more discouraging when you are finally able to quiet that chatty part of yourself, and in turn don't know what to do next. The problem with us human beings is that we have been programmed to think too much, to analyze everything that we do, to dissect it into tiny little pieces until we look at them under the microscope of endless insecurities. What we need to do is cover that microscope up and put it away. The best way to quiet the mind is to distract it like a child with a new toy, give it something to keep it busy. Guided meditations are the way to go, and the good news is that there is a plethora of options these days. Whether you download a free app or find them on the internet, the possibilities are endless. Start with the intention of quieting the mind by listening to a guided meditation every night for 10 minutes. There is an abundance of categories to choose from, whether it be for relaxation, stress reduction, insomnia --- you name it, there is a guided meditation for it.

One reason guided meditations are so helpful is because they take the guesswork out of relaxing. People get so stressed out about whether they are meditating correctly that they become more stressed than when they started. The important thing to understand is that there is no right or wrong way to relax. Everyone operates in a different way. We enjoy different foods, follow a preferred lifestyle, have different desires. The point is that no two people are the same, therefore, there is no wrong way to meditate. The goal of the meditation is to promote relaxation, balance and peace, so that your body can take a break from the stress hormones running through the body. The first step in doing this is to disconnect from that pesky *Nemesis*. Cut the cord in those 10 minutes, so that there can be peace and quiet in your energetic field. Your heart rate will lower, your breathing pattern will change, your muscles will loosen up, and you will feel absolutely at peace - even if only for a few moments a day. Trust me, your body will thank you for it, and the more you do it, the easier it will be. It will become routine, like breathing and eating. Meditation will become part of your daily routine --- so much so, that you will notice a difference, and even a slight shift if you don't do it for a period of time. Remember that our body is incredible in that it is designed to ensure that we continue living. Despite the circumstances and external changes, your body is durable and stubborn. The body's goal is to retain homeostasis, however it can. It will figure out a way to adjust to just about anything within reason. This means that if you train your body to relax daily and put an effort into promoting balance within your body, both physically and energetically, it will re-adjust its homeostatic threshold to compliment your new lifestyle. Unfortunately, if you fall off the routine, your body can easily fall back into old patterns, in order to adapt to your mindset.

Emotional High Rise

Your Intuition is like a muscle, the more you work it out, the bigger it becomes. Just like anything in life, to be good at something takes practice and a desire to see it through. To strengthen your connection, you must raise your vibrational frequency, and meditation is just one way to do that. To understand vibrational frequency and how that relates to your wellness, you can use the analogy of an elevator system. Imagine a beautiful high rise with 100 floors. If you break apart the building into decades, we can think of these decades as emotional states of being. The very bottom decades are the floors that house the lower vibrational emotions, such as fear, anger, resentment, guilt, jealousy, and hate. These floors should be avoided as much as possible. However, should we find ourselves on one of these floors due to an argument or a traumatic event, we must do what we can to go back to the elevator as soon as possible and press the up button. We can get on that elevator as soon as the light turns on and the door opens, or we can hang out in the vestibule in contemplation and self-pity for as long as we want. It's our choice. Because the lower floors are dark and dense, sometimes we may become trapped there and perhaps influenced to stay. Maybe some of the rooms on those floors are filled with old romantic partners that were never good for us, or estranged family members that caused us pain at some point, or even a set of acquaintances who we thought were friends, but, in time, we realized that they only drained us, and selfishly kept us there with them for their own satisfaction. These floors may be filled with trauma, pain, disease, disappointments, and the sides of our self that we wish that no one would see. We may try everything to get off of those floors, but something is drawing us back there. Perhaps it's that *Nemesis* again, pulling you back, to keep you in this illusionary comfort zone, out of fear of taking a chance on another floor. There are many who remain stuck on these bottom floors for a variety of reasons: their parents never made them feel good enough, they failed too many times in life, they had no self-confidence, they were overweight and used that as poor leverage of self-worth, or they suffered depression. Those people most severely affected become consumed with anger, allowing their *Nemesis* to hold them hostage.

When we are stuck on these lower floors, we may have physical symptoms of fatigue, headaches, backaches, insomnia, and worse, cancer. This is because when our vibration is low, we are in a dense energetic environment. This causes a disruption of Chi in our body, and the energy that would normally flow in and out with ease through our meridians and chakras now ceases to function properly. This can make it very difficult for us to move, let alone find the elevator. We become desperate, and we may begin to manipulate others into thinking we are on the same floors that they are on. Spending the day participating in activities where we put on a facade, a fake version of our self that everyone expects of us --- and undoubtedly finding ourselves back on our lower floor at the end of the day. We may also deceive ourselves and deny the floors exist altogether. Wherever we land on the spectrum of reality, the important thing is that we put our energy and effort into finding the elevator, so we can finally make the choice to move to a higher floor.

Let's move on to some of the other floors. Think of the Twenties, Thirties, and Forties as pit stops on our way where we make forward progress or backtrack. If we find our self somewhere in the middle of the building, we are likely living a complacent, yet dull existence. The good thing about these floors is that if we are moving up, we are slowly raising our frequency, which gives us the motivation and inertia to keep going in the right direction. We may have little boosts of energy, moments of happiness or a glimpse of hope, all the while encouraging us to reach higher and higher. I would guess that the average person is somewhere in the middle decades, hovering around the floors that have become their comfort zone. Since they are safe, friendly, and possibly well received, we may easily become long term tenants on these floors. The rooms may be brighter, there may be more accommodations, and more modern amenities; why risk losing it right? Here lies the conundrum. We become stuck in our own fear of needing more, we desire and strive to be better, and yet are unsure of how to begin moving up to another floor. What if my furniture doesn't match the tone of my new room? What if nobody likes me up there? What if I don't fit in? What if I fail and take a giant leap back down to the trenches, the lower levels, the land of the misfits? Do you hear your negative talk? These are the voices of doubt coming from that long-lost *Nemesis* that you thought you sent packing. *"Get out!"* you say to yourself, *"I thought I told you to leave me alone."* This can play out in one of two ways: we can either cave in and succumb to our shadow side --- we might as well press that elevator down button --- *or,* we can kick our *Nemesis* back to the curb, take a deep breath, collect our thoughts, realize it's

OK to have these worries and make the conscious choice to release them - all of them.

When we start to move up the floors of our wellness journey, our mindset begins to shift. We feel lighter, more secure, and more confident. Our pace becomes fluid and free. We may even feel as though we are gliding. The higher the decades in the high rise, not only support that mindset, but they encourage it, as though each decade simply leads to the next like a secret passageway. As you release those emotions that no longer serve you throughout your transition, you will find it easier to move from floor to floor, as if you are leaving your unwanted baggage behind. When you settle into higher decades, your emotions will shift, you will feel happiness unlike you have felt before, love will take on another meaning, and you will be filled with joy and excitement. As you travel through the Seventies, Eighties, and Nineties, you will find them to be magnificent and life-changing with the most rewarding and exclusive floor finally within your reach - the penthouse. The penthouse is where we should all strive to be. I am not referring to a multi-million- dollar penthouse in New York City. I am referring to your inner penthouse, your spiritual awakening, your transformation that leads to more than *You*.

The penthouse is the place where we use our new found enlightenment to help others. It's a place where we can spread our light and change lives by helping people elevate and travel up their own personal high rise. This is truly what it's all about: elevating the planet and changing perspectives through the transformational process, so that we can all evolve and change the trajectory of humanity. If we can all play our part, and take our individual healing journeys to transform and evolve into better, more compassionate people, we can really make a difference.

Here are some examples of your High Rise emotions associated with the decades

High Rise floors	Emotional state of being
Penthouse	Peace, Love, Joy
90	Happiness, Abundance, Serenity
80	Clarity, Confidence, Gratitude
70	Relief, Security, Pleasure
60	Complacency, Reflection, Consideration
50	Contentment, Satisfaction, Contemplation
40	Exhaustion, Weariness, Doubt
30	Fatigue, Confusion, Uncertainty
20	Guilt, Worry, Jealousy
10	Fear, Anger, Resentment

Once we are comfortably settled in the higher floors of our high rise, we are then able to make a viable connection with our Intuition. When we are in a place of peace and balance, we can connect more easily. When we are operating at a higher energetic frequency, we are able to break away from our *Nemesis.* There are other ways to establish a connection with your intuition, such as mindful breathing, visualization and releasing. Mindful breathing is a powerful mechanism to relax your entire body. Breathing is a natural way to re-boot our system, so that our bodies can be brought back to homeostasis. This is one of the most effective ways to relax in the hardest moments. Breathing is our body's natural way to release, not only carbon dioxide, but also energetic buildup. When we breathe mindfully, we can intensify the process exponentially. I started using a progressive breathing technique when I needed to relax. I referred to this method as 3-5-7. It works by taking a breath in for three seconds, holding it for five seconds, and releasing for seven seconds. Any variation of this works, as long as it is a progressive inhale, hold, and release. I teach this technique to pregnant women in my childbirth classes. The reason this type of breathing is so effective at calming your body is because it allows for the oxygenated blood to stay in the body for moments longer, lowering the heart rate, blood pressure and generating a feeling of peace and calm. As a society, we are walking around in fight-or-flight response mode almost daily because we are constantly running from one task to the next. Our bodies are not designed to be in this adrenaline-based mode as often as we are in modern society. The result is that we are unable to sleep and relax in the moments when we can. This is because our bodies are attempting to adapt to this lifestyle of fight-or-flight we have created, resulting in imbalance. When we relax our body with progressive breathing, we quiet our mind, thus opening that door to our Intuition. Once the door is open, you will have the opportunity to ask your Intuition just about anything.

Visualization is another way to access your Intuition. Try creating a safe place that you can go to, and imagine that the safe place holds the door to your Intuition. Let's say that your safe place is a quaint little cabin in the woods. It's a small rustic one-room cabin, with a fireplace and a small bed, just big enough for you. It's warm and safe. Only you know where to find it. Visualize yourself going to that cabin to escape your mind, your *Nemesis*. Allow yourself to sit on the bed, gazing at the fire, imagine the sound that the fireplace makes: it crackles and pops, and it makes a beautiful bouquet of orange and red. This place is so relaxing that you can go there as often as you need. It only takes a moment of your imagination. In fact, all you have to do is close your eyes, and you are there. Within this cabin is a ladder on the wall that appears to lead to a skylight. Visualize yourself climbing up the ladder and opening the hatch to the skylight. To your surprise, as you pass through it, you are taken to another place. This place can look anyway you desire, as long as your intention is to connect with your Intuition. This place could be on the moon, in an enchanted forest, in a canoe on a lake. Wherever your imagination takes you, follow it, and allow this place to be your direct connection with your Intuition. Once you identify this place as the place you can connect with your *Friend*, begin to ask your *Friend* questions. Pause and listen to the answers you receive. The answers can come to you as words, visions, or thoughts. They can be painted in the sky with clouds, come as flashes of pictures, or could be your inner voice whispering to you ever so gently. No matter how the answers come across, be open to them, and, more importantly, don't second guess them. One of the most challenging parts of our spiritual growth is trusting the answers, visions, and messages that we receive. Our *Nemesis* gets involved and becomes a third wheel, feeding you doubts, making you second-guess the information that you are receiving. You begin an active dialogue with yourself, your *Friend,* and your *Nemesis* about who is right and where the messages are coming from. This leads you down a path of hesitation, causing you to feel a little nutty and discouraged.

Think of your *Nemesis* as your annoying sibling who will stop at nothing to come into your room when your friends are over. No matter how many times you kick him out, he keeps coming back, louder and louder, banging on the door. One way to lock your *Nemesis* out of your safe space during your mediations, or when you are attempting to communicate with your *Friend*, is to create a place to put him. One thing that I did when I was first figuring out ways to reach my *Friend* was to leave my *Nemesis* in a wooden box, within an imaginary closet, with a lock which only I had the key to. I would relax my mind, do some progressive breathing, and on my way to my safe place, I would envision a door that led to a small utility room. I would leave unwanted emotions, theoretical baggage, and my *Nemesis,* in that place. I would place my *Nemesis* inside the wooden box, and close it tightly. I would talk to my *Nemesis* and explain that I was leaving him in there so that I could go on my journey, and I would pick him up on the way back. I would close the door, lock it, and go on my way. As much as I have spoken poorly about our conscious mind, our *Nemesis*, it does serve a purpose --- in times when we are truly in fight- or-flight, to help us make quick decisions, and react in times that we don't have time to think. When we need aggressive and quick thinking, when we need to react quickly in a car to avoid an accident, when we are in a traumatic situation where we are being attacked, we need to act fast to get away. In those situations, our *Nemesis* is our built-in security system, so we don't want to lock him up for good. We just need to know how to put him aside in the moments that we need to make the most important decisions, when we are trying to connect to our emotional support system, our *Friend*, the one that is looking out for our long-term well-being.

Strengthening your Connection

Once you have established a connection with your Intuition through your safe space, you can strengthen the connection by visiting frequently. I recommend purchasing a journal, one that is devoted to your spiritual growth, to keep track of the messages, visions, and guidance you receive. I always recommend to my clients to keep track of all meditations, visits to their safe place, and dreams they have. Write the date, what you are doing (meditation, dream, random vision while driving), and write down everything that you can remember. Often times when you look back, you will notice themes and small clues that don't make sense individually, but, when combined have a message. It will be difficult to do that based solely on memory, so make it easy for yourself and keep track with journal entries. You will thank yourself later. Another benefit of keeping track is to measure your progress. You may start out with smaller clues through flashes of images, or words that pop in your head, and through time, these words turn in to sentences, and the flashes turn in to wonderful scenes. The important thing to remember is that the progression can be slow, so have patience during the periods of blank space, and be grateful during the periods of abundance and flow.

One thing that I learned all too well is that Spirit will guide you within their time frame, not yours. The funny thing about time is that, here on Earth, it is such an important part of our society; it keeps things moving along on a schedule. We are programmed to base our entire day on that countdown of how many hours are left. The frustrating thing is that we create lists for ourselves that we need to accomplish in any given day. Our day gets filled with an abundance of tasks that, in a perfect dream world, we would like to get done to satisfy ourselves by checking things off. However, in reality, there is no way we can get to half of it. This is our *Nemesis* setting us up for failure on a daily basis. When we don't feel satisfied with what we have achieved, we in turn look at ourselves like a failure, ending up in this never-ending cycle where every day begins in the same place of low vibration, and then feeds into each next day at exactly the same low vibration, until we simply give up.

Don't give up!! When you have those days where nothing is working for you, and no matter how hard you try you can't seem to connect and your safe space has seemingly disappeared and is out of reach, remember that your safe place is quietly stored in your subconscious. I assure you that it has not gone anywhere. If you are having difficulty finding it, your connection is weak, and you have somehow slipped down to the lower levels of your high rise, it's okay. Give yourself a break, be kind to yourself, press that elevator-up button, and make a choice to remove yourself from that lower vibrational state. Forget the safe space for one night, and concentrate on just breathing. Take slow, mindful breaths over and over until you feel yourself rise, literally until you feel lighter, as though your body is floating, and so relaxed that your muscles loosen, the grip of your jaw loosens, and you experience a feeling of calm and peace once again. Simply enjoy that experience for as long as you can because the important thing is to recognize when your vibration has lowered, to take note of it, and to quickly make the choice to bring it right back up. Close your eyes and visualize yourself pushing the elevator up button, imagine it illuminating, and the door opening. Press the level that you desire, that is within your reach, and feel yourself rise up until the elevator stops and see yourself going through the door when it opens.

Thank yourself for being strong and wise, for having the courage to rise back up again, even if you didn't feel like you could. The more and more you make the effort to rise up, even if it is multiple times a day, you will notice your progress and your wellness and healing journey will become easier. You will get to a point where you don't need the elevator anymore --- you will just rise with no effort at all.

Chapter 2
Relax: Understanding How Emotions Affect our Well-being

Now that you understand a little more about how to tap into your Intuition, let's take some time to talk about how emotions *really* affect our well-being. When you experience a lower vibrational emotion (one from the lower decades of your high rise), the energy attached to that emotion enters the body through the chakra which correlates with that vibration. When a person is balanced and operating from the higher decades in their high rise, they allow the emotions to pass through, immediately recognizing that they don't like the physical response to that emotion, whether that be a rise in heart rate, tensing of the muscles, uncontrolled shaking or knots in the stomach, they immediately release it. They don't want to feel those symptoms anymore, so they choose to let it go. The energy attached to that emotion passes in the body and right back out again, no harm no foul. Unfortunately, the vast majority of us are not able to do that, because we are either living in the middle decades of our high rise, making it difficult to release emotions easily, or our *Nemesis* creeps back in and encourages us to remain angry, to marinate in the energy it brings, and use it for fuel to fight back. As a result, that negative energy becomes stored in the body and becomes trapped.

Each time you get into an argument, or experience a traumatic event, all that emotional baggage stays in the body if not released. Take a moment to look back at all the times in your life from childhood that you didn't make the effort to release the emotion associated with the event --- either by brushing it under the rug, ignoring it and refusing to talk about it--- over time, your body becomes inundated with trapped emotions. Your body can only hold so much of that energy until it reacts; your body gives you those subtle signs of distress, to get your attention, to let you know that something is not right.

Sometimes a good cry or exercise can release some of the trapped emotions, but crying or exercise doesn't release the trapped emotions entirely, these physical responses may release a sliver of them, only taking the edge off in the moment. Many people are walking around like ticking time bombs of emotions, causing them to overreact or become overwhelmed in situations that wouldn't normally have that effect on them. Parents, for instance, may carry those trapped emotions from decades of living. They go to work and have a stressful day and come home to children who are full of energy and looking for their attention. At such times, a child's slightest misbehavior can cause an unreasonable reaction from the parents, resulting in a blowup over nothing. Unfortunately, the guilt associated with that episode of overreaction just adds to more trapped emotions, piling them up more and more. These trapped emotions and their energy become unwanted house guests in our bodies, which can lead to chronic issues, diseases, and cancers. The more trapped emotions we are harboring, the heavier the burden we are carrying. The illustration on the next page shows how the body can feel while trapped emotions stay in the body. We can feel weighed down, dense, fatigued, and our immune system will be operating at a low level.

Illustration of the weight of our emotions on the physical body

Trapped Emotions

What we need to do is release these trapped emotions once and for all. If you are like most of us, you may have more trapped emotions than you are aware of because you may have suppressed these emotions so deeply in your body that not even you can find them. This is true for many of our childhood traumas. Using their natural built-in survival instincts, children have an incredible ability to suppress and forget about their traumas. They either release it immediately, or for those extremely traumatic life events, such as abuse, they pack it away tightly. The problem is that it tends to resurface in adulthood in the form of anxiety and instability. Because the memories have been buried so tightly, the person has no recollection of the event. Only the emotion is left behind. Many people end up in therapy in search of the root cause, desperately trying to figure out why they lack confidence in their life. This is where things become really tricky because, if the person can't identify the source of their pain, there is no amount of therapy that will help them make the connection between the emotion and the event. They end up focusing on the triggers that cause the emotional reaction and, in turn, try to avoid those triggers. This is much like taking a pill to alleviate pain instead of figuring out why there is pain to begin with. It's a temporary fix, and if I have learned anything about trapped emotions and their energy, it is that until they are truly released, they will find a way to resurface until you resolve them and become free from their energy.

Emotional Spring Cleaning

It is important to simply relax in this part of your journey. Think about the emotional baggage that we carry like a closet full of things we have stored throughout the year. They are the piled up dusty items that we have collected that really serve no purpose, so they become this disorganized mass taking up space. Then spring comes along and we become motivated to clear it all out, to make room for the new, sorting through the mess and getting rid of our junk, like spring cleaning. In that initial period of feeling overwhelmed by the massive amounts of stuff to go through, there is initial panic, then the feeling of possibly putting it off for later follows. But once you relax and decide to take on one item at a time, your thoughts shift from anxiety to motivation. We need to move away from our trepidations of releasing emotional baggage and towards excitement and enthusiasm for the process. Relaxing is the first step. This may seem like a simple and obvious first step. However, it can be quite difficult to relax when you are feeling overwhelmed and anxious because, in those moments when you have slipped back down to the lower levels in your high rise, it becomes more challenging to relax. Before even thinking about all the energetic emotions that you have trapped inside your body, before you allow yourself to become overwhelmed, start by setting an intention that you are going to take it slow and steady, leaving room for breaks, and that you are going to conquer this *energetic closet* at your own pace.

Let's talk about how to relax for a moment. You have to train your body to relax on a routine basis, so that relaxation is not a foreign concept. You can set an Intention to relax for 10 minutes a day, either in the morning or evening before bed. You start by finding a comfortable space in your home. It can be your bed, a comfy chair or a space you designate as your "relax zone." I created one of these spaces in my home by claiming a corner in my bedroom. I went out and bought a comfy dog bed. Don't judge. They are very comfortable. I also bought a few soft throw pillows, and added one of my favorite Buddha statues and some crystals (this is optional of course). You can add anything to your space to make it more comfortable and symbolic of relaxation. I dedicated that spot to my meditations, journal entries, and reading books. I knew that this was my own personal space that no one else in the house would use, so only my energy surrounded it. When I used the space for relaxation, I would sit comfortably with my legs uncrossed (keeping your arms and legs uncrossed is important to keep the energy flowing). I would close my eyes, and do a few minutes of progressive breathing to help my body relax. Throughout that period, I would notice my mind wander and begin to list the things I needed to do instead of relax, such as preparing dinner, making lunch for the kids, and doing the endless laundry that was calling out to me. I would simply allow those thoughts to flow in and out of my mind until I felt myself succumb to the relaxation.

A few examples of what I would experience physically during those periods are weightlessness, tingling sensation throughout areas of my body and even the extreme opposite of feeling heaviness in my body. When you elevate your vibration, you literally rise energetically, and you can interpret that in one of two ways. You can feel light and free, as the muscles in the body relax and release their tone, or you can feel the opposite, heavy as though your body is a ton of bricks. This phenomenon is because you are literally feeling the weight of your body as you rise above it. It really doesn't matter which one you feel, there is no right or wrong, the important thing is that you are relaxing. Once you have brought yourself to a relaxed state, you can then remain in that space with no other Intention than to relax. Your body will thank you for it. Our bodies are looking for opportunities to relax other than during sleeping hours. Even taking breaks during your stressful workday and doing a few minutes of mindful progressive breathing outside, in your car or even the restroom, will do wonders for your well-being and state of mind. Breathing is a helpful form of release without having to think about what it is that you are releasing. The Intention in the moment is to simply relax the body, so that it has a chance to take a break. Just like you need a break during the day from your job, your body needs breaks from having to think, act, and defend. When your body is going at full steam all hours of the day, it pulls from its energetic reserves that your immune system needs to fight off viruses and bacteria that attempt to invade your body when it is weak. Because we tend to push our bodies to the point of sickness, our energetic fuel tank is on empty a majority of the time. When this happens, we are less likely to be able to connect with our Higher Self or our *Friend* when we need them the most. It's almost like trying to take a cross-country road trip on one tank of gas.

Learning to find ways to balance your energy is the first step in your Wellness Journey. Relaxing is an important part of balancing. If you do not relax the body, your body will not be in balance. The more you allow your body to relax, the more you will be able to tap into your Intuition. Your Intuition will be your best friend on this journey --- so clear off the front seat for him or her, and get ready for a fascinating ride.

Chapter 3
Recognize: Identify Emotions and Stressors Contributing to Your Disharmony

To identify your trapped emotions, you must first recognize whether they are your emotions or someone else's. In order to explain this more effectively, we need to go over what our energetic bodies are. Since we are all energetic beings, we have an energetic field that begins immediately outside our bodies and expands outward up to 7 feet away from us. Depending on our emotional state, the energy coming from our body varies. Emotional states of fear, anger, and resentment are lower vibrating emotions, so the energy that we put out in our energetic field will match that. The higher-vibrating we are, the more expansive our energetic field can be. That is why it is important to be mindful of your thoughts because you don't have to say anything out loud for your energetic body to react.

The thoughts and emotions that we have internally reflect outwardly whether we are aware of it or not. Since our energetic field expands past our physical body, the energy we give out is what is perceived by other people. For example, when two bodies come close to each other, it is the energetic bodies of the two people that meet first. Long before there is a physical connection, such as a hug or handshake, the energetic fields are merging together, feeling each other out. If person A is aggressive and angry, the energy he or she is giving out is dense and low vibrating. If person B is happy and balanced, their energy is high vibrating and light. When person A and B come towards each other and their energies meet, Person A will feel unsettled near person B, and they may not even have a conscious explanation for it. They may be meeting for the first time and person A is put off by person B before they even talk to each other. This is because our energetic bodies always meet first. Some people are more sensitive to the energies and are able to detect when someone else's energy is either negative or positive. When you go into someone's home and their dog is either really friendly with you and in your face, or reserved and reluctant to greet you, it is because they are master energy readers. Because they can't communicate through words, their other senses are heightened, one of which is to assess the energy of a person to know if they can trust them. This doesn't always mean that if the dog doesn't like someone, the person is bad. It just means the energy that the person is emitting, in the moment, is unpleasant to them, causing them to react to the person. Having a stressful day at work is enough to make your energy disorganized and unbalanced, and it can be interpreted as negative in the moment. Our energies can fluctuate throughout the day, as often as our emotions fluctuate. This can make our energetic body ever changing. Depending on the moment, we can be vibrating high and then back to low in a matter of seconds.

Energetic Bodies Meeting

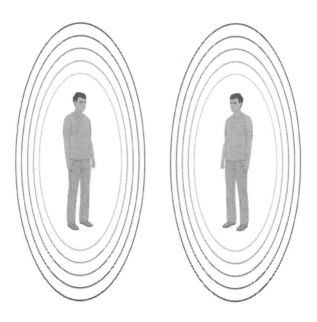

It is important to recognize your energetic body. That awareness will enable you to be mindful of how your emotions and thoughts will affect it. Another important reason to understand how emotions affect our energy is to become aware of how the energy of another person's energy can affect you. You can be operating from a place of balance and peace, and come in to contact with someone who is aggressive with an energy body reflecting that energy. If you allow it to mix with your energy, it can bring your energy down to match theirs. They can literally bring you out of your balanced state because your energy mixed with theirs. If you are unaware of how to protect yourself energetically, it can take you by surprise. If you have ever been out running errands and you felt completely wiped out when you got home, that is because you came into contact with a variety of energetic bodies, some of which could have drained your energetic battery.

Protecting your Energetic Body

Learning how to shield your energetic body is life changing. There are a few different ways to shield your energy, and it starts with your Intention. Once you get ready to leave your home in the morning, set your Intention that you are asking the universe to surround your energetic body with a shield of protection. It can be in the form of white or golden light. Imagine you are completely surrounded by this light on all sides, top to bottom and that you are in a bubble of light. Depending on your beliefs, you can ask for a higher spirit or angelic being to provide that shield. You can call on Archangel Michael, God, Kuan Yin, Mother Mary, or Saint Germain. It can be anyone you desire. If you are not sure who to ask for, simply ask the Universe to provide you with the highest vibrating shield of protection. What that does is protect your energetic body when you are around others, so that it is not vulnerable to lower vibrating energies. More importantly, your energy will not be susceptible to being drained by others.

The mirror method is something you can use if you are in a toxic environment, and you need another layer of protection. You would first place your golden bubble around yourself, and then ask that an energetic mirror be placed around your body, front, back and sides. This will cause any negative energy that is directed towards you to be reflected back to the person that sent it. This is especially important if you have a toxic workplace where there are a lot of negative, competitive people. Those people tend to have a lower vibration and can send out negative energy without consciously being aware of it. It is simply a side effect of the energy that they are giving off or surrounding themselves with. You are not sending negative energy back their way. You are simply reflecting their negative energy away from yourself and back into their energy field.

Another effective protection method is to ask that Saint Germain invoke the Violet Flame around your golden bubble. This is a powerful transmuting light that dissolves anything that comes your way. Just think about a true flame of fire: anything that comes near it will burn to ashes. This violet flame is so powerful that any lower-vibrating energies you come into contact with will dissolve as soon as they reach the violet flame. This is a powerful energetic blocking mechanism that can be used daily, especially when you are unaware of the energy you are surrounded with. You don't even need to ask for Saint Germain if you are not comfortable. You can simply ask for the violet flame to surround your body and it will.

Protecting your energetic body is one of the most important parts of your balance routine. It is simple and only takes a few minutes a day. If you forget to do it before you leave your home, just do it as soon as you remember. Remember that we are all energy, and as our energetic bodies move up our emotional high rise, we become lighter and brighter. We literally have a beacon of light that illuminates our spirit, and this can be quite attractive for lower vibrational beings. The brighter we are, the more susceptible we are to an energetic attack. Lower-vibrational energies try to dim our light. The reason we are attractive to the negative energies of others is not important --- just understand that it is imperative that you protect yourself every day if you want to remain balanced. This is especially important when you are attempting to communicate with spirit, or doing meditations. Always protect yourself.

Energetic Shield of Protection

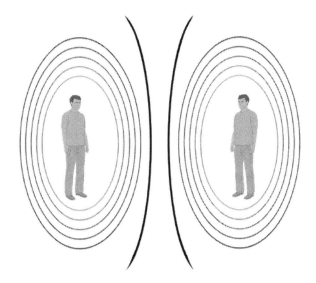

Protecting your Children

Children have some of the most vibrant and dynamic lights there are. This is because they are so connected to the spirit realm, having been on the Earth for a short time. Because their light is so bright, children have some of the most attractive energies. As parents of these children, it is recommended that when you are protecting yourself each day, that you include them as well. Whether you are protecting them from other energies at school when you are not around, or when you are together, remember to protect and shield their light. When you have young children who seem to act unusual or perhaps at an extreme to their normal personality, take note of it because it could be that their energetic bodies are distressed from all they came into contact with that day. They may not be acting themselves because their energetic bodies are tapped out or mixed with a variety of other energies that are not their own. Remember to include your children in your protection routine daily.

The Power of Attraction

Most people have heard of the power of attraction, where you attract what you put out energetically. This is because whatever your vibrational energy is, it will attract similar energies to its field. If you are optimistic and joyful, you will attract that type of energy towards you, and you will thrive in that environment. Whereas, those people that are anxious and frustrated will attract people that are similar energetically. Have you ever noticed those people who always seem to have bad things happen to them are continuously in negative situations, and, in turn, have a negative opinion about almost everything? Those persons, whose energetic bodies are vibrating low and dense, draw negative energy. They attract negative people and negative situations to them like a magnet. Be mindful of your thoughts and your words, so that you can attract the type of people into your life who are uplifting and contribute positive energetic vibrations. If you catch yourself in negative self-talk such as, *"I can't do this,"* or, *"I will never be great,"* you are setting yourself up for exactly that result. What you say, what you think, what you visualize will reflect back to you. You have the ability to manifest greatness, and in the same manner, to manifest your negative words and thoughts. A vital part of your wellness journey is to make it a point to surround yourself with those people who lift you up, who have good energy, who make you want to do better and be better. In turn, you will mirror that behavior and inspire others to follow their dreams, their true purpose.

Clearing your Energetic Body

Now that you understand how emotions affect our energy, and thus affect what is attracted into our life, it is equally critical to learn how to clear your energy. Most of us have busy lives, with long lists of tasks to complete. It is easy to forget to protect ourselves, especially in the beginning before it becomes as routine as brushing your teeth. Be patient with yourself, and if you forget, just do it when you remember. Even if it is in the middle of the day, take a moment to visualize the shield and ask for protection. It is never too late.

If you find yourself feeling fatigued and drained, more so than usual, it is possible that you have what I like to refer as *energetic garbage* attached to you. It is inevitable that all of us have unwanted energy hanging out in our auric field at some point. Once we recognize that it is there, we can clear it away with our Intention. Even if you are unsure if you have unwanted energy attached to you, it doesn't hurt to clear yourself. I will go through some easy ways that you can clear your energy field.

Cleansing Shower Meditation

This is one of my favorite meditations, and you can do it every morning or evening. When you are in the shower, imagine the warm water running over your body is clearing your aura of all unwanted and negative *junk*. This is a simple meditation that relaxes the body and mind.

In your mind, ask that the water cleanse and purify your energetic body back to balance, and ask that all energy attached to you that is not of your highest good be washed away and taken down the drain. Allow yourself to relax, loosening any tension in your body as the water flows. Set your intention to release, release, and release.

Waterfall of Colors

This meditation is one that I use frequently on my clients when they come to me for an Energy Session. It is a simple way to cleanse the Aura of unwanted energy with the use of colors. This meditation should be done in a comfortable position. A few minutes of progressive breathing can be done first in order to relax the body.

Close your eyes, and visualize that you are in a beautiful forest: imagine the trees, the ground beneath you, the sounds of birds in the distance, whatever your imagination reveals to you. Visualize walking towards a beautiful waterfall flowing into a body of water below, only this waterfall is full of beautiful bright colors. All the colors of the rainbow are flowing down the waterfall. There is a ledge that you can walk on that takes you right under the flow of this waterfall of colors. Once you visualize yourself standing under this waterfall, visualize that, as the colors wash over you, they are cleansing your Aura of all unwanted energy. As the colors flow, allow yourself to release and relax. Once you have spent enough time under the waterfall, when you feel Intuitively that you are done (3-5 minutes), walk away from the waterfall. Now visualize a beacon of golden light coming down from the sky between an opening of trees a few steps away. Stand under that golden light and allow yourself to be energized by the Universal Light. Ask that it replenish you and surround your entire energetic body, giving you a boost of love and light.

Setting an Intention to Clear

One of the simplest ways to Clear your energy is to ask for the Universe to help you. You can request that whomever you feel comfortable with, whether your guides, Angels or simply the Divine Universe, to Clear your energetic body of all that no longer serves you, and ask to be surrounded with energetic vibrations which are of your highest good.

The method you choose to Clear yourself is not important, as long as you commit to doing it periodically or making it a part of your daily routine. Use your imagination and come up with your own method of Clearing. Our imaginations are limitless, so allow your Inner Child to come out and assist you in creating your own unique clearing ritual.

Section Two: Transformation

"Yesterday I was clever,
so I wanted to
change the world. Today I am wise, so
I am changing myself"
-Rumi

Chapter 4
Releasing

Now that you are able to tap into your Intuition, and you have the tools to recognize your ability to take control and move up and down the levels of your Emotional High Rise, you are ready to release the emotions holding you back from achieving greatness. A large part of the Transformational Process is making lifestyle adjustments, and making the commitment to healing yourself is the first step. In order to transform like the butterfly, we must first shed the parts of ourselves that are no longer needed. As we evolve, we must release all that serves no purpose for the greater good of our life. Once we become free, we leave our cocoon and spread our wings and fly wherever the wind takes us.

There are many ways to release trapped emotions in the body, if you are aware of the emotions that you have been storing in your body, then the process will be easier. Let's first discuss the many ways we can contribute to storing negative energy in our body.

Negative Self-Talk

This is one of the most common ways that we become entrapped in our emotional baggage. We succumb to negative self-talk without realizing just how detrimental this can be. Most of us have thought negatively about ourselves at some point in our life. Think back to when you said something like, *"I can't do this,"* or, *"I'll never get first place,"* or my personal favorite: *"I am such an idiot."* I say it is my favorite in a facetious manner because that is what I used to say to myself when I made mistakes or did something embarrassing. It seemed harmless at the time, a typical response following an act of regret. However, compounding these negative thoughts can lower our vibration instantly, and the energy that we suddenly surround ourselves with will mirror that. When we are in a negative mindset, directing that negativity inward, our bodies will respond accordingly. We may feel tired, have less energy, and little motivation to do anything. Countless studies have been done on the power of words and their effects on two plants growing in the exact same environment - same soil, same amounts of sunlight exposure, and clean water - with the only difference being the verbal stimulus each receives. On a daily basis, while one person is speaking positive uplifting words to one of the plants, another person is saying negative destructive words to the other plant. In nearly every study, the plant receiving positive and encouraging words would flourish, while the other plant, given negative and limiting words, would wilt and nearly die. Words have power. Even if you don't say them out loud, your body still responds and reflects that energy outward whether you realize it or not. If someone is angry and has negative thoughts and is placed in a crowd of happy balanced people, unknowingly the others would likely navigate away from that negative person without even realizing it. This is because the energy bodies of the group negatively affected by the energy being projected by the angry individual, so their bodies naturally gravitated away.

Have you ever noticed that when you are in a negative mindset, bad things just seem to happen in clusters? Again, this is an example of how the energy you put out into the world attracts similar events that replicate it. Until you can bring yourself out of a negative mindset, you will be vibrating on the lower floors of your High Rise, immersing yourself in that energy --- you will remain there until you choose to press the elevator up button, to get you up and out of it. It's that simple. We have a choice. We are in control of our mindset and who and what we surround ourselves with.

Now that you have a better understanding of how negative self-talk directly affects your well-being, you can move forward in a more mindful way. The next time you have a negative thought, recognize it and make a conscious choice to release it. Follow it with something positive, so that you immediately go back up to the higher floors and don't become trapped. For example, you didn't get the promotion at work and you are feeling defeated and frustrated. These are normal emotions to have especially if you have been working hard to get that promotion for years. It is OK and necessary to allow yourself the opportunity to feel what comes naturally. It's what you do next that counts. Once you have gone through the negative thoughts, make a choice to let those thoughts go. They serve no purpose, and will only keep you in that negative frame of mind. Take a deep breath. As you exhale, say in your mind that you are releasing those emotions; follow that up with uplifting, motivational thoughts such as, *"Something better is coming for me,"* or, *"I am excited for new opportunities."* This will bring you back up the levels of emotions quickly and effectively. Once you put that positive energy out there, it will attract to you positive opportunities which you may not have even thought of.

Shadow Side

Think of your Shadow Side as that part of yourself where your *Nemesis* lives. Your Shadow Side is comprised of all the negative experiences you have had in all of your lives, and of all the times you did anything bad to someone else. An accumulation of that energy is stored in your energetic make-up, and lies dormant until called upon when we are in a negative space. Everyone has a Shadow Side - even the best of us. The difference is how much of that Shadow Side is in control. I like to use the example of a pie chart, where 90% of the pie is our transparent True Self, and 10% is our Shadow Side. This percentage can certainly shift from moment to moment depending on what is happening in our life. For example, the Shadow Side of an abused child can build up a little bit at a time. With each abusive event, the Shadow Side becomes bigger. In severe cases of emotional or physical abuse, the child grows up to have a large percentage of his pie chart taken over with the Shadow Side. This is because he never felt safe or loved, and lost his true sense of self in the process. This can lead to that child becoming an adult with destructive patterns because they are operating from a place where the Shadow Side is in control, encouraging him to do bad things to himself and others because he is programmed to believe that he is not good enough. He is living with a pie chart that is essentially flipped. His Shadow Side is now 80- 90% in control and his True Self is in control only 10-20% of the time. He is living with a feeling of loss, resentment, anger and no self-confidence, which only fuels the Shadow Side. Although this is an extreme example, it is all too common for the Shadow Side of many people to fluctuate by as much as 30-50%, causing them to have destructive patterns and a low sense of self-worth. This makes it very difficult for these people to be successful and, more importantly, happy. Try to keep your Shadow Side in check, so that it doesn't run your life. To keep the Shadow Side at a small sliver on your pie chart, release negative thoughts and remain in the higher levels of your emotional High Rise.

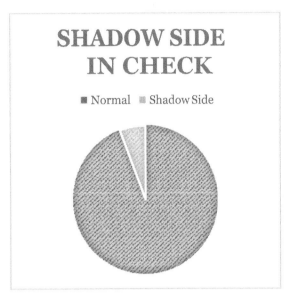

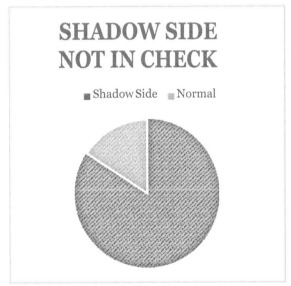

Forgiveness

One of the most effective ways to release negative emotions is to forgive. Many of us hold on so tightly to the anger we feel for someone who has done us wrong. We sulk in that anger and marinate in it until we become saturated and overcome. People often come to me with situations where they are: victims of sexual abuse, are angry with a spouse that had an affair or are angry with friends that did something unspeakable to them. They are in victim mode and unable to move out of it. They proceed to list the many reasons why they can't forgive the person, all the while validating their anger and grief. Many people refuse to forgive because they are not finished punishing that person just yet. In their eyes, the act was too painful to forgive. Another common reason is that they feel that if they forgive the person, then they are ultimately excusing the person for what they did and thereby, giving them a free pass. What I say to those people is that they are correct in the way they feel because that is their reality, their truth, and their emotions. However, by remaining in that state of anger, they are binding themselves to that person who abused or hurt them and to that experience, as though time has stopped. I tell them that they will remain in that moment as long as they choose. The abusing, hurtful person has likely moved on, freely living their life without conscience, and you are still stuck in that moment, frozen in your own anger. I inform people that forgiveness is not about giving anyone a free pass. It's about choosing to free yourself and your energy from that moment and that space.

We are not excusing anyone from doing horrible things. What I ask of you is that you excuse their soul for the awful act that their body did. Let me explain this a little further. Many of you have heard James Van Praagh say that we are all souls having a human experience. When we come into this world as a baby, we have a clean slate. Some believe that you can come into a new life carrying traumas from past lives in the form of cell memory. Simply put, the subconscious stores those memories, which can carry over into the present life. An example of this would be a person with an irrational fear of drowning in the ocean with no real reason to have such a fear. He or she could have drowned in a past life. The trauma associated with that experience comes through to his or her next life. Anytime they go near the ocean, they have a negative reaction. To make things simple, let's just assume that each new earth life comes with a clean slate. Whatever happens to this person as they grow either contributes to a positive life experience or a more difficult one. We have not witnessed all the moments of a person's life, all the times they were hurt, abandoned, treated poorly or didn't receive love. We can't comprehend the demons that a person carries with them due to traumatic life experiences that contribute to their negative behavior. When this person hurts another, whatever the action may be, we have to think about what caused them to do the hurtful action. Perhaps they grew up in an environment of no love or support from their parents, causing them to grow up feeling as though they are not good enough to receive love. Their Shadow Side is likely in the driver's seat of their actions, and they hurt others because they feel hurt. This does not excuse their behavior. However, it is helpful to look at them in a more compassionate manner as we don't know the path they walk. It doesn't always have to be such a severe example. Sometimes, a child grows up in a household where, no matter how much they achieve, in their parents eyes it's not good enough. They grow up in an environment where the bar of success keeps moving up every time just as they reach it, and they spend their lives trying to reach a goal that is not achievable. Because they are in competition mode most of the time, they may do things to put themselves ahead of others with no thought or concern for others. Whatever unforgivable act has been done to you, try to step back from the situation just for a moment, so that you may grasp the bigger picture. Pay attention to other factors, or reasons that this person did such a terrible thing to you: are they unhappy in their life, jumping from relationship to relationship in fear of commitment? Do they shut people out in fear of rejection? Do they hurt others to fill a void of deep unhappiness, not wanting others to be happy and fulfilled because they are not?

Once you have taken a moment to reflect, next imagine that person as a soul, not as a person. Because we are all beautiful souls that come from light, we are pure, compassionate, and filled with an abundance of love. When we come down to Earth with that clean slate that I mentioned, it is up to our life experiences and how we allow them to affect our overall well-being that dictates our ability to forgive. If we stop looking at each other as humans and look at one another as souls living in this dense atmosphere of endless challenges and doing the best we can, we may be able to forgive in a different way and with greater ease. When faced with the choice to forgive someone, try looking at forgiveness as an opportunity to forgive their soul, their Higher Self which would never intentionally hurt you. I stress the word choice because we ourselves dictate the length of our sorrow and trauma until we are ready to release it. We are not giving them a free pass for what they did. Instead, we are empowering ourselves by setting our energy free from theirs, cutting the cord that binds our energies together. Forgiving someone for their actions is both liberating and transforming. It not only frees you, it also expands your compassion for others through truly understanding the tremendous challenges that these souls, having a human experience, endure.

Meditation for forgiveness

After a few minutes of progressive breathing, imagine yourself in a beautiful healing room. It can appear any way you desire --- with beautiful lights, angels, flowers, moon and stars --- whatever comes to mind. Then, visualize yourself standing in that healing room with the person you are forgiving standing facing you. Next, think about that person as a soul --- not just as the body they are inhabiting. They may have a beautiful aura around them. They may shift in some way to reveal their true essence. Take a moment to tell the person how they have hurt you, allowing all of the emotions to come forward. Then visualize an energetic cord connecting the two of you together. This is an unhealthy, negative cord filled with the all the emotions associated with your connection. Next, tell the person that you forgive them for hurting you because you understand that it came from a place of weakness, and you know that their soul is pure and good regardless of what they did to you. Tell them that you are choosing to cut the cord between you, disconnecting you from this pain they have caused you to free both of you once and for all. Next, imagine a powerful white light, almost like a lightsaber, cutting through the cord and severing it completely. When the cord is cut, visualize it dissolving into the white light. Once you no longer see the cord, imagine a beautiful pink light surrounding your body, sending you love, peace, and calm. Watch as the same pink light spreads over the other person, giving them the same love as their soul needs the healing as well. When you feel you have received enough of the pink light, say goodbye to the other person, and watch as they disappear. Once they are gone, thank the universe for assisting in this healing, and open your eyes when you are ready.

Releasing Trapped Emotions

When emotions become trapped in the body, physical ailments will occur. They normally start superficially, like a small rash on the skin. This is because our skin is the first entry point to our body, so it acts as a protective barrier. Whether the energy is trapped inside the body trying to get out or the energy is trying to get in, the skin will become affected. Another first symptom of energy disruption is headaches. They occur suddenly and may go away once the emotion is released. If not, they will re-occur or worsen into migraines until the emotion is released. Other minor alerts your body gives you that you have energy trapped in the body that needs to be released are stomach aches, diarrhea, eye twitching, back or neck pain, heart arrhythmias and hypertension. These are all acute signals that your body gives you to let you know that something is wrong. When ignored, they can re-occur until they manifest more severely as Fibromyalgia, Irritable Bowel Disease, Crohn's disease, Parkinson's, Alzheimer's, and Cancer.

There are many different ways to release trapped emotions and the energy associated with them. The important thing is that you make the effort to release them, so they don't cause harm to your body and your well-being. I recommend trying all of the methods before deciding which one works best for you.

Muscle Testing
Muscle testing is one of my favorite ways to receive answers from your subconscious. It is a simple technique to access the guidance you seek from a place of truth and honesty, without reservation. Your muscles are directly connected to an energetic grid that flows in and out of the body. When there is

truth and harmony flowing through the body, the muscles will remain strong. If your body detects something that is notgood for the body, the muscles will essentially short circuit and weaken momentarily as the negative energy runs through. This is why people who suffer from depression or are constantly surrounded by negativity, feel weak and fatigued. You can take this intricate system of electrical impulses and use it to access answers that are guided by what's best for you. If you are trying to decide what food is best for your body or, for example, whether you have a sensitivity to gluten, you can use the muscle test to find out how your body will respond to it. If you get a positive response, you know that your body is not sensitive to gluten. If you get a negative response, you know your body is trying to tell you to limit your gluten intake. You can perform muscle testing to receive answers for just about anything, especially to find out if you have trapped emotional energy in the body. You simply ask the question, *"Do I have trapped emotional energy in my body with regard to anger, fear, guilt, or sorrow (or whichever emotion comes to mind)?"* Make a list in your journal to keep track of the questions you ask and the answers you receive.

How to muscle test yourself

The easiest way to muscle test is to use the sway method. Stand firmly with both feet on the ground, and both arms on either side hanging loose and relaxed. Make a truestatement, such as, *"My name is..."* After you say your name, notice how your entire body starts to lean forward. This is a positive response. Your body is letting you know that is truth, and it leans in a forward direction. This is believed to happen because, most of our lives, we operate in a forward motion. We receive food with the front of our bodies. We sit in front of a computer to work. We walk forward. We move towards things we like. If we make a false statement, such as,

"My name is Jane," or any statement that is not true, notice

how your body begins to shift slightly backwards. Your body is answering you by telling you, *"No, that is not a true statement."* Once you have discovered your baseline, you can begin answering more questions. If this method doesn't work for you, try using your hands. With your non-dominant hand, put your thumb and your index finger together to make a circle. Have them touch and remain strong in their position. Next, place your other hand's thumb and index finger inside the non-dominant hand's circle to make two circles which are connected. Hold them strong, and pull your hands apart, while keeping the circles together, a few times to get the hang of it. Next, ask your true statement, and attempt to pull the circles apart. You will not be able to pull them apart for true statements. If the statements are false, the dominant hand's circle will break through.

Practice both methods a few times before deciding which one you like the best. There are other ways to muscle test, such as using your full arm, or your fingers, or using a pendulum. In my opinion, these two methods I have described are the easiest to learn.

Sway Method

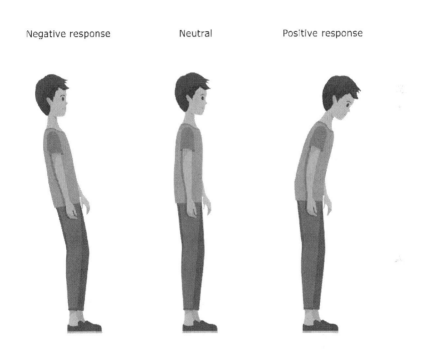

Negative response   Neutral   Positive response

Finger Method

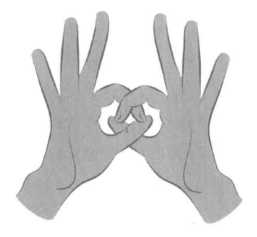

Once you have identified which emotions are trapped in your body, set an Intention to release them as they no longer serve your highest good. You can simply say that you choose to release the emotion. Place one hand over the top of your forehead with your other hand over your heart, and take a few deep breaths. As you exhale, release the energy through your breath, imagining the energy leaving your body each time you exhale. You can inhale and exhale as many breaths as it takes until you feel the release. Then muscle test to find out if the emotion is gone. If it is not, ask a series of questions to identify what else you need to do to achieve the release. You may need more time to breathe through the release or you may need to muscle test to identify how old you were when the emotion first got stuck in the body. Once you figure out that age, think about what was happening in your life at that time and identify the original event. Now ask if it is time to release. If yes, repeat the release process by placing one hand against your forehead and the other over your heart, and allow your exhales to release the energy from your body. Because this is an incredibly powerful process, it is strongly recommended that you only attempt to release a few emotions per day to allow your body a chance to rebalance once the energy is released.

Emotion Code

Some emotions are buried so deeply inside that we are unaware that they are there. These emotions can be embedded in areas of our body which are oblivious to us. This is because at the moment when they were attached, we did not realize the extent of our sorrow. Even the most seemingly minor incidents can have an impact on our emotional well-being. If we don't process them in the moment, those emotions can become attached as well. They may resurface years later, completely unexpected, and take you off guard. The easiest way to identify whether you have trapped emotions is to use Dr. Bradley Nelson's method called the Emotion Code. You simply use muscle testing in order to locate the emotions using a chart. Once you have identified the emotions, you can follow his process to release each emotion. The process is simple enough that a child could do it, and the effect is profound. This is a great way to identify trapped emotions of which you are unaware. Visit http://www.drbradleynelson.com for more information on The Emotion Code.

Emotional Freedom Technique
This method was created by Gary Craig in 1995 and can also be referred to as the Tapping Solution. By tapping meridian points on the body, you can release stored emotional energy. It is different than emotion coding in that you tap the meridian points while thinking about a traumatic event. The thoughts will bring the emotions to the surface. The tapping motion will clear them by breaking up the energy. While tapping, you stimulate the amygdala, the part of your brain which can trigger the fight-or-flight response, thus making it a powerful and effective form of release. The process involves bringing up an event or emotion that you want to release and consciously thinking about it while you tap your body's meridian points --- the release is immediate. By releasing the emotions this way, pain, anxiety, and the emotional energy associated with the traumatic event can be nearly eliminated. This simple method is free, easy, and available to anyone willing to try it. For more information on how to do Emotional Freedom Technique (EFT) visit https://www.emofree.com.

Other Ways to Release

Journaling

Writing is an effective way to release, and many artistically-inclined individuals prefer this method. That is not to say that you need to be a good writer for this method to work. You simply must enjoy the process of writing out your thoughts. First, identify the trapped emotions you feel, such as low self-esteem, worry, anxiety, doubt and fear --- list anything that comes to mind that you want to release. Then list events in your life that may have caused these emotions to become embedded in your body. Think as far back in to your childhood as you can remember. Once you have your two lists, you begin releasing one emotion at a time. It is best to work on only two to three per day to allow your body to process the release. Use a new page of your journal for each day, writing the date and the emotion at the top of the page. For example, if one of your emotions is guilt, write that at the top of the page. Sit with that emotion for a moment, close your eyes and allow yourself to see what comes to mind. Perhaps memories may begin flowing of times in your life when you felt guilt or witnessed guilt. It can be one experience or many. Once you begin to have flashes of memory, write them down. Write everything down that comes to mind. Don't stop writing until you have nothing left in your mind that relates to that emotion. Pay attention to any physical response you may have to the emotion, such as butterflies in the stomach, crying, or shaking. Whatever it may be, allow your body to react organically. There is no right or wrong response. Write down your physical responses as well, in order to keep track and, later, identify themes. After you are done writing, decide once and for all to release this emotion from your body, as it no longer serves any purpose, and is likely preventing you from going up the levels of your High Rise by weighing you down.

Meditations to Release

Utility Closet

This meditation is for those individuals who are more analytical and feel a need to be in control of their healing and releasing. Start by doing a few minutes of progressive breathing and ask to be surrounded with protection while you do this meditation. Visualize yourself walking down a hallway. It can look any way you wish. It can have many doors on either side. Walk down the hallway until you find a utility closet. Open the door and enter the closet. Inside, there may be mops and brooms, or whatever your imagination reveals to you in the moment. Visualize a box in the corner of the room, pick it up, take off the lid, and with focused Intention, release all that you want to rid from your mind and body in the form of visions, words, and thoughts. Imagine all that you intend to release is being placed in the box, one after the other. Continue placing emotional energy into the box until there is nothing left to release at that time. Remember, you can come back the next day and release more. Next, place the lid back on the box, and put it back down on the floor. Imagine that there is a key in your pocket. Leave the closet, pull out the key, and lock the closet door. Take a moment to look at the closet door you have closed. As you focus on the door, allow it to disappear, until there is nothing left. Lastly, visualize yourself flying like a bird over a large body of water. When you feel ready to release once and for all, drop the key into the water and visualize it sinking out of sight. Give yourself a few moments longer to fly in the sky and feel light and free, not weighed down by all those emotions you were holding on to. Note anything that you feel afterwards --- euphoria, tingling, or lightness --- in your journal.

Angels Release

This meditation is for those who are more spiritually inclined and prefer the assistance of an Angelic presence. Start by doing a few minutes of progressive breathing and ask to be surrounded with protection while you do this meditation. Ask that your Angels are present before you begin, to ensure that they are given permission to assist you. Make sure to ask for the highest vibrating Angels to assist in your healing to eliminate any chance of lower energies interfering. Proceed by visualizing yourself walking into a beautiful dome of divine light that is a vibrant gold or white. Allow yourself to walk through the energetic barrier until you are inside the dome. Once you are inside, an Angel greets you. If you can't visualize an Angel with a physical body, just feel their presence. The Angel will come close to you and open your crown chakra just above your head with her hands. Ask her to assist in the release of all emotional energy and trapped emotions in your body at that time. Feel her begin to pull the energy out of your body through your head, as though her hands are a vacuum, pulling out energetic blockages from your body. You can contribute by asking that certain things be released or simply trust that all that no longer serves you is being released. You can stay within the dome of light for as long as it takes until you feel the pulling stop or she closes your crown and steps back to let you know that the clearing has been completed. Next, imagine that the dome you are in suddenly becomes illuminated in a bright white healing light. Allow your body to be saturated by this beautiful healing light as it flows through and around your body, filling the spaces that you just released with a rejuvenating powerful all-encompassing light from the Universe. Stay in this light as long as you need. When you are ready to leave, go through the dome until you are outside of it and open your eyes.

Hot Air Balloon

Start by doing a few minutes of progressive breathing and ask to be surrounded with protection while you do this meditation. Visualize a beautiful large hot air balloon in front of you. Imagine all of the colors and design of your balloon. Allow yourself to get into the basket. Once you are inside, it begins to rise. You travel over beautiful mountains and valleys, or whatever comes to mind. You look down and notice that there is a box on the floor of the basket you are in, open the chest and place all emotions, events, fears and anxieties that you want to release. When you are done filling the box, close the lid and imagine that you are now over the ocean traveling low enough that you are not far from the ocean surface. When you are ready to release the emotions, pick up the box and toss it over the basket and into the ocean. The ocean is a beautiful turquoise color where you can see through the water below. Watch as the box sinks. The ripples of water at the surface carry away emotional residue, and your box sinks to the ocean floor. Immediately, you feel the balloon rise slowly up high in the sky as the weight of those emotions being released allows you to rise, elevating you to a place of clarity and peace. Stay floating in your balloon as long as you wish, saturating yourself in this newly found freedom and calm.

These are all simple and helpful meditations for releasing known and unknown negative emotional energy from the body. Don't feel pressured to release your whole life's emotions in one meditation. I recommend you do a little at a time, so that your body has a chance to process each release. You can start with small categories and do a new meditation every other night. It is important to be patient and to give your body a chance to catch up with the release. After breaking up the energy that has been trapped inside it, the body needs to adjust and rebalance itself. Some side effects from this process can include mild fatigue, crying, vivid dreams, or random thoughts of previous traumatic and emotional events in your life. Whatever happens, be patient, and don't resist. These side effects are the body's physical and conscious reactions to residual energetic fragments that are slowly breaking away and releasing. Your body will need rest and sleep to regenerate. Drinking more water, and eating whole, high-vibrating organic foods through the process will aide in your body's recovery.

Exercise

Incorporating a low-impact exercise routine into your meditations and release work is important because exercise increases circulation and releases endorphins, which can aid in your mental well-being. Three to four days a week is all you need in order to make a difference and see a shift in your mental and emotional state. Activities that raise your heart rate, increase your breathing, and increase the circulatory process throughout the body are not only physically beneficial, but also energetically supportive. Through perspiring and increased breathing, energy stored in the body can break up and be released through the exhaling and sweating process. The escalated circulation ensures the energy in all areas of your body are reached for maximum release. You should discuss your exercise routine with your doctor first to ensure that you are doing the right form of exercise and avoid any injury to yourself. Ask your physician before including any new exercises to your routine.

Walking is soothing to the soul, as it doesn't require too much physical output, but the results are impactful. When you walk, especially outdoors, you can allow your body to connect with nature, which is beneficial to both the body and soul. Walking is a form of meditation --- as you might have noticed, sometimes you can easily become lost in your thoughts. That first level of relaxation is called Beta when the body begins to relax by way of daydreaming or drifting off in thoughts. While your mind is distracted, your body has the ability to rebalance with each step you take as your heart rate and circulation slowly rise in harmony with each other. As you exhale, you release energetic build-up that has been slowing you down. If you can walk through a pathway of trees, the oxygen that you breathe in can be rejuvenating. This is a great way to exercise without putting too much pressure on the body, especially if you have restrictions on physical activities. Allow yourself to walk. Set an Intention to release unwanted energy with each exhale.

Running is another great way to release, speeding up the heart rate and accelerating the energetic breakup more quickly than walking. The higher your heart rate, the more energy is released, leading to more endorphins in the body. This will rejuvenate your body and promote a more productive day. Running is one of the most effective ways to release lower-vibrating emotions, such as fear and anger. Trapped energy is broken up as the circulatory system speeds up, reaching more cells in the body. Deeper breathing and sweating that accompanies running intensifies the exhalation, which is how the energy leaves the body.

Swimming or floating in the water is a powerful method of release, as the buoyancy of the body when submerged in the water is both freeing and calming. Whether you swim laps or simply float in the water, the process of dulling your senses while in the water is a powerful combination. If you have ever stayed underwater for a long breath, it is a peaceful feeling. As the frequency of sound shifts, your muscles relax, and the body calms down. You don't even need to elevate your heart rate. Just being in the water is soothing for the body.

High Vibrational Meals

It is no surprise that what you put into your body directly affects your energy and health. High-vibrational foods encompass anything grown or produced with love. Vegetables and fruits grown on a farm, with no pesticides, nourished by happy farmers will produce vegetation that will nourish the soul. Vegetables that are mass produced, covered in pesticides, or grown in a lab, will not provide high-vibrating nutrients. Cows and chickens that are raised on a farm, given high quality grains, with the opportunity to roam free will produce better milk and eggs. Animals that are raised for food can imprint their emotional trauma into their bodies. When we eat their meat, we consume the negative energy that was trapped inside them. Animals raised with respect will not leave negative energy in their bodies for us to consume. If there is a lot of negative, low-vibrational energy in the meat we eat, our bodies will have a difficult time digesting it. If we have a stomach ache after we eat meat or a feeling of heaviness or intense emotion, it could be a sign that our bodies are reacting to the emotional disturbance of the meat.

There is little positive nutritional and energetic value with consuming processed foods. Because we live in a society where we are constantly running behind schedule, we have minimal time to feed ourselves the right type of food. High-vibrating, quality ingredients are both expensive and take time to prepare. Oftentimes, it is easier to grab something from the pantry than to prepare a healthy meal. This is especially true for parents with picky eaters where the focus becomesgetting them to eat versus eat healthy, fresh, and organic.

If you want to incorporate a more nourishing diet into yourlife, buy organic whenever possible, especially meat. I would rather cook meat less often during the week than buy store brand meats. As a mother of three, I find it difficult to budget a healthy diet, especially when processed foods are less expensive. For busy lifestyles, meal prepping is another way to ensure that you eat healthy during the week. If you wait to figure out what to cook when you get home from work, you are more likely to cook something quick and easy, which isn't always the healthiest option. However, if you meal prep your healthy options, you can have quick easy meals every night. If buying organic creates a hardship, simply bless the food and feed as much positive energy into the food you are preparing and eating. This will increase the vibration. Giving thanks to the Universe for your food and cooking with love and grateful thoughts, can certainly elevate the positive energy in your food. Being mindful about your diet is key. If you provide your body with the right food, you will allow your body to remain balanced, keeping your immune system strong, and thus raising your vibration.

Chapter 5
Realigning and Rebalancing our Mindset and Thought Process

At this point in your healing journey, you have learned how to tap into your Intuition and identify and release emotional energy that is holding you back. The next step in the process is learning how to balance your mind, body, and spirit to enable you to move forward in your transformational process with confidence. Becoming a more mindful, compassionate, and connected person takes commitment, perseverance and patience. There is no quick fix or pill that can be taken to accelerate your transformation. There may be days that you fall back into old patterns, bringing you plummeting down your high rise and making it feel impossible to pick yourself back up again. It is imperative that you grant yourself a pass once in a while for these setbacks to prevent discouragement and feelings of failure. The most important thing to remember is that although you fell off the boat, you have the tools in your theoretical floaty to get you back on board again. Don't forget all your prior work. Call upon your *Friend* to guide you back up, motivating you to find your center and balance once again, so that you can keep moving forward. Many people I have worked with have become discouraged in the beginning of their healing journey because they realize how much conscious effort is required to put themselves first for once. It takes courage, and there may be backlash from others who chime in and give their opinion about what you are doing. I believe we should all invest as much in ourselves as we would anything else. The payoff is far greater than putting ourselves last, as many of us do, which perpetually drains our energy and clouds what it is that we truly want. We tend to get lost in a sea of everyone else's needs and lose sight of what makes us happy, what our desires, and dreams are. I understand this all too well, as a mother, wife and fur mom. I would put myself last, always making sure everyone else's needs were fulfilled before my own. It became an obsession, and over took my existence. I am filled with an abundance of love for them and only want the best for them. I thought that meant they needed all of my attention, all of me, if I was to be the best mom and wife. I became drained, tired and ultimately cranky, which led me to be the exact opposite of the *perfect* mom I aspired to be. It wasn't until after the birth of my third child when I was feeling completely overwhelmed and drained that I had an epiphany: I had to make a change or I wasn't going to make it much further at the pace I was going without getting sick, or worse, contracting a terminal illness. Once I changed my thoughts, patterns and priorities, I saw a shift in myself. My energy and my capabilities enhanced. I was more balanced and became an even better mother.

Note to Empaths

Being an empathetic soul in today's world can be both uplifting and challenging at the same time. We have more and more empaths currently walking this Earth because we are in a time when we need their energy and compassion the most. The conundrum is that because we have so much negativity on the planet right now, empaths are struggling and drowning in their sorrow for others. They watch the news and see mass shootings, people dying, corrupt politics and their hearts are bursting with emotions --- they are feeling everything as if it is their own tragedy. Empaths are capable of tapping into the emotional struggle, pain and suffering of others, as if it is actually happening to them. They have this ability because they are tapping into the universal consciousness, with which we are all connected. Everyone's soul is connected to the Universal Intelligence, an electromagnetic field that vibrates with all living things. All of us have the ability to tap into this collective, but our vibration and frequency needs to be high enough to make this connection. Think of the higher levels of your High Rise. The higher the floor you are on, the easier it will be to tap in. Empaths have a natural ability to tap into the universal oneness of all humans, animals and living things. They feel with their soul, they connect on an individual level with those in their presence as well as those on the other side of the world. They have a difficult time turning this ability off. Sometimes to their detriment, they become overwhelmed with their compassion for others. They respond to other people's souls, auras, and true selves. They want the best for everyone, even at the expense of their own well-being.

If any of this rings true, you are likely an empath. We are in great need of more empaths at this time, to rebuild our collective consciousness and to remind mankind that although we may be walking different paths, we are all connected. If you are an empath, remaining balanced can be a difficult part of your journey. You have an important job to do, and it is important not to lose sight of your own journey while caring so greatly for others. Be sure to shield and protect yourself every day. Release all that is out of your control through daily or weekly meditation and understand that change takes time. We are on an evolutionary shift to higher consciousness, and patience is paramount. Don't let others dim your light. Continue to shine brightly through the darkness. Don't lose hope. Use your light as a beacon of serenity to guide all others who come into your path.

Reevaluating What's Important

A large part of the process is reevaluating your needs and wants, shedding your life of all that no longer serves you. Take a moment to assess what is important to you. Write it down in your journal. What is happening in your life that contributes to your desires --- a supportive husband, positive and uplifting friendships, financial stability, or possibly a job that feeds your soul and gives you purpose? These are the things that are working for you, contributing positively to your life. Give gratitude for whatever is on your list. Even if it is just one thing, it is something to be valued and recognized. Then spend some time thinking about what is holding you back from achieving greatness, whether that is an unfulfilling job, pessimistic friends, parental expectations, pre-programming of what is socially acceptable and possibly your own doubts. It's time to start eliminating things from your list that are holding you back. Start with things that are feasible, such as shedding negative friendships.

Evaluate who you are surrounding yourself with -- are they positive, uplifting and supportive, or judgmental, negative and jealous? Every few years it is a good idea to do some spring cleaning of the people in your life too because they directly affect your balance and well-being. You may be a very positive person, but if you surround yourself with people who are chronically negative, you will begin to notice that you become saturated in their negativity, making it difficult to rise above it. I evaluate my friendships on whether there is an even exchange of energy - do they help me as much as I help them? Positive friends contribute to your life in a positive way. They are there for you when you need a hand, a shoulder to cry on, or motivation to be better. A good friend is there for you when you fall and lifts you back up, encouraging and inspiring you to become the best version of yourself. These are friends that you want to cherish and be grateful for. You don't take advantage of them, and you reciprocate the same beneficial energy that they send to you.

A friend who is chronically negative, impulsive in his or her decisions, and insecure at others' success is not the type of person you want to surround yourself with. When you are clear-headed enough to recognize who your true friends are, it is time to release those that no longer contribute to your life in a positive way. This does not mean they are bad people. They just need to surround themselves with like-minded people until they are ready for their own transformation. Everyone is at their own pace and shouldn't be judged for their speed. The process of elevating our planet and building bridges of compassion and kindness for all to benefit and prosper is not an individual race, but rather a unified mission. We are all walking our own journeys. Some paths may be clear of debris. Others may be filled with rocks and sticks. The important thing is to support one another as we are all moving in the same direction. When you are in the process of weeding out friends, be kind to them and wish them the best.

Material items is another area of life that needs to be evaluated. Take a moment to reflect on what is important to you. Then look around at all the material items you have collected over time. Ask yourself if they contribute to your well-being or if, perhaps, you obtained certain items because you felt you needed to blend in with others. Purging yourself of material items that fill no purpose other than to take up space in your home or to satisfy others, should be considered an important and routine ritual. Consider donating old books, antiques, and clothes that you no longer use. Decluttering is a powerful form of release, as we hold emotional energy in our physical materials, which is not always positive. Get rid of the things that hold bad memories, that remind you of difficult times, that serve no purpose, and that only add to the collection of negative energy in your home. It is equally important to clear your home of lower energy that surrounds physical items, as well as energy in the open space of your home. Think about when you come home from a challenging day. You may be stressed and agitated. When you take off your coat and hang it up on the hook, you are also dropping off some of the energy that you are carrying around and setting it free to roam around your home. The unwanted energy that attaches to your auric field, or energetic body, can settle into your personal space like an unwanted houseguest. When you declutter your home, set an Intention to clear the space by lighting a candle, opening some windows and asking that the universe remove all lower-vibrating energy from your space. Take control of your home and demand that it leaves. Using a smudge stick is another way to clear your space. As the smoke rises, it takes the energy along with it. Follow that clearing by asking the universe to surround your space with protection to limit future negative energetic tenants from moving in. The more you clear yourself and your home and request protection, the less vulnerable you will be to the unwanted energy around you.

Disconnecting from Pre-programming

Much of our life is spent absorbing what the world thinks of us, how our parents mold us, and what our friends like about us. That projection can mask and cloud our true sense of self. As we navigate through life as a toddler, a teenager, and a young adult, we are constantly receiving input from outside of ourselves about how we act and think. Depending on whether those reactions are positive or negative, we subconsciously begin to mold ourselves in ways to surround ourselves with those positive responses, which in turn shapes who we become. As we enter adulthood and prepare to go out into the real world, we feel lost and insecure because many of those who shaped us throughout the years are no longer present. We are left standing alone, wondering who we really are. I believe people come into our lives for a purpose, whether to teach us something, or to take us out of our comfort zones. It is important to recognize that those who seem to walk into our lives once, at just the right time and only for a brief moment, can make as large of an impact as our parents, family members, and long-time friends. Experiences with those that cross our paths will either shape us into better people or perhaps will make us realize that we don't want to be a certain way. The important thing is that we make those determinations from a place of balance and self-worth.

Back to Balance

Being balanced is a relative term. It can refer to many aspects of your wellness. Your mind, body, and soul thrive in a balanced energetic system. When the energy flow throughout the body is efficient, the body will be able to function at an optimal level. When we are balanced, the immune system is strong. The chakras are spinning with ease. Our aura is filled with bright light. We attract positive experiences and people into our life. Our emotional state of mind has a lot to do with how well the energy is flowing around and inside the body.

Balancing Chakras

Chakras are the energy centers just outside our body that allow the energy to flow into the body and back out again. There are seven main chakras that dictate this flow. Each chakra relates to physical body functions and the emotions that match the vibration of each chakra. You can think of the chakras as the security system for the energy flow of the body. They control what energy comes in and out, based on what is best for the body at the time. Chakras function like mini fans that extend a few inches from the body. When they are working efficiently, they flow in a clockwise motion, allowing an appropriate amount of energy through them. When they are functioning at a lower capacity, they are either spinning clockwise, yet very slow, or they reverse and spin counter-clockwise. This means the flow is disrupted due to an outside stimulus, such as another person's lower-vibrating energy coming through and shifting the system or from a lower-vibrational event, such as an altercation that causes a large amount of negative energy to flow through and throw everything out of balance. If this event or energy is vast and the person doesn't process it, or release the energy from their body, the chakra can stop all together. The fan stops running and no energy is coming in or going out. Although this is an extreme case, it is extremely common. A good majority of clients who come to see me have at least one chakra that is blocked due to events or traumas in their lives. These blocked chakras need immediate attention. Otherwise the lack of natural energy flow can cause physical illnesses, such as irritable bowel disease, severe acute back pain, stomach ulcers, and cancers. Let's go through the chakras to better explain where they are in the body and what they relate to.

Root Chakra

This chakra is located at the base of the spine. It is the foundation where our body connects with the Earth and the world around us, and is the life-force energy that fuels all of us. Our physical connection, sense of stability and security and feeling of safety and support reside here. Our fight-or-flight reflexes and primal parts of our Self operate through this chakra. This chakra represents all that is physical, including our tactile relationship with the world around us --- what we touch, feel and the physical sensations of our bodies. If these experiences are positive, the chakra is open and flowing with ease. If we are put off by something, such as pain, it can close up to protect the body. This is where our *Nemesis* lives and is fueled by our deepest fears and regrets. If we are generally grounded and balanced, this chakra is flowing smoothly and freely. If we are scared, frustrated, angry and anxious, the flow will be disrupted. The physical symptoms that may follow can vary from hip pain, lower back pain, and colon and lower bowel issues.

Sacral Chakra

This chakra is located just below the navel, and represents our sexuality, artistic, and creative expression. This chakra is more emotional than tactile, it's the part of our awareness where we consciously recognize that there are other people in the world besides ourselves. Having meaningful relationships with others are driven through this chakra, allowing connection with others in a more mindful and emotional way. We begin to expand our awareness of other people's happiness and needs. Creative sparks and expression are heightened and showcased through this chakra. It is the place from which we feel free to broadcast our unique essence and unique personalities and desires. If this chakra is not functioning to its true potential, we may lack artistic expression, creative drive, and the desire to fulfill our life purpose. As such, our motivation to be the best version of our self and to accomplish greatness will diminish, which can literally stop us in our tracks. Our physical body may experience kidney, bladder, lower intestinal, and female reproductive complications. If women come to see me because they are having difficulty becoming pregnant, this is one of the first chakras I assess.

Solar Plexus Chakra

This chakra is located just under the sternum, near the belly button. It represents our personal power and is our connection to the Earth and the Divine, the in-between of two worlds colliding together. This is one of the most powerful chakras, as it feeds us confidence, empowerment, compassion and that *"fire in the belly."* If you have ever had a *"gut feeling"* about something, you were tapping into your solar plexus, which just so happens to correlate to the stomach. This is our emotional center, where we either process our emotions, or block them out. This chakra truly fuels the body and motivates and drives our soul to fulfil our purpose. Most artistic people who draw or paint are tapping into the wisdom of their solar plexus, where creative sparks and expression manifest. If this chakra is not flowing well, you will feel fear, judgement, lack of motivation, and anxious. Some physical symptoms include fatigue, stomach pains and ulcers, liver disease and pancreatitis. When this energy center is working at its optimal potential, you will feel like you can do anything you set your mind to, you will be filled with excitement, confidence and empowerment.

Heart Chakra

This chakra is located in the middle of the chest at the level of the heart. It encompasses all aspects of love, whether that be love towards others or love towards yourself. When we experience hurtful moments in our life, we sometimes place energetic walls or barriers around our heart to protect our heart from getting hurt again. This could be one experience, with a small barrier, or many experiences with a wall so thick that nothing can get in or go out. Our subconscious does all that it can to protect our heart because, despite what people believe, our heart is our most important organ. It feeds our energetic body and connects us to the Universal Consciousness or the connectivity to all living things. The electromagnetic field that comes from our heart is vast. The subconscious protects it like the secret service protects the President. Many clients who come to see me have a blocked heart chakra because they give out an abundance of love to everyone in their life, but don't allow love to flow back into their heart. For various reasons, they feel they don't deserve it. Their heart wall blocks the love from entering all together. It is so important to love yourself and accept yourself first before you can love others in a healthy more balanced way. For the heart chakra to flow appropriately, it requires a balanced flow of love in and out. When it becomes unbalanced, the heart chakra stalls and starts to spin counterclockwise or it will stop flowing altogether. Some physical symptoms include heart flutters and arrhythmias, asthma, pneumonia, chest pain and, in more severe cases, heart attack. Make a point to analyze the flow of love in your life, and how balanced it is. If you are the type of person that gives out love, yet doesn't allow it in, or tends to hold grudges and anger towards others, then your heart chakra is likely blocked.

Throat Chakra

This chakra is located in the area of the esophagus and trachea, near the thyroid. It is responsible for your ability to express yourself through words and verbal communication. If you are able to express yourself to others without fear of ridicule and judgment, you have a healthy throat chakra. If you have trouble talking to others and saying what is on your mind, or if you hold back your thoughts out to fear or politeness, this chakra will not be functioning properly. As humans, we have been given the gift of verbal communication. There are no other creatures that communicate using words. Animals use sounds and tones, but not words. In order for this chakra to flow appropriately, we need to follow our truth by voicing our opinion and express our uniqueness through the sound of our soul. If we hold back for too long, we develop physical symptoms of acid reflux, coughing, tonsillitis, sore throat and laryngitis. Enabling ourselves to talk to others respectfully, standing our ground and sharing our opinion, is an important aspect of being human. Communication is a valuable tool that can be complex and awkward at times. However, it can also be incredibly satisfying and enriching. It is an extraordinary gift.

Third Eye Chakra

This chakra is located between the eyebrows, and it directly connects us to our subconscious and our Intuition. This is where our *Friend* lives and thrives. When we tap into our Higher Self, we are utilizing this chakra. The stronger the flow, the more connected we become. This chakra also connects to the pineal gland, which is located in the brain and regulates melatonin and serotonin. Many people believe it is the link that connects us to the spirit world. The more active the pineal gland, the better connection we have with our guides and angels. Many clairvoyants have an active and healthy third eye, which assists them in their connection with the Divine and tapping into others' energy fields. If you have an active imagination, vivid dreams of the future, strong Intuition and sensitivity to others' energy, your third eye is likely flowing very well. If you are closed off to your ability to imagine anything other than the present, and you have doubts about your Intuition, your third eye may be blocked or flowing in the wrong direction. The third eye is an important part of our senses, as the root chakra is for survival. This chakra is about wisdom and passion, dreaming into the future, and manifesting all that we desire.

Crown Chakra

This chakra is located just above the head and channels our direct connection to the higher realms of reality. This is a powerful chakra in that it drives our universal life force, our connection to Spirit, and the Divine. This is the pathway to our higher consciousness where pure joy and happiness are experienced. When we open ourselves to the Spirit realm, beyond the physical aspect of our reality, our extrasensory awareness heightens. The crown chakra is the integration of the whole being - the mind, body, and soul. This is the highest level of human expansion and is our evolutionary process. When we block our belief and openness that there is more to this world than our eyes can see, this chakra will be blocked all together. When we deny this aspect of our consciousness, a part of our soul lies dormant. It doesn't diminish or go away. On the contrary, it longs to blossom and be free. Physical symptoms of a blocked crown chakra are migraines, nervous system imbalances, fatigue, poor vision and neurological issues. The emotional effects are depression, lack of desire, feeling disconnected and isolated, and difficulty connecting with others. When we allow ourselves to tap into our innate ability to connect with the higher realms of reality, it is both enlightening and expansive. Our awareness and experiences are nourished by our connection with Spirit.

These illustrations show where the chakras are in the body, and how energy flows

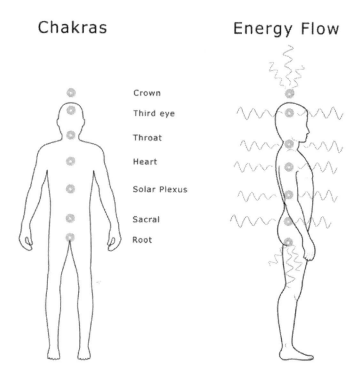

Chakra	Color	Location	Body Part/System	Balanced Emotions	Unbalanced Emotions
Crown	White/Violet	Top of Head	Brain Pineal gland Eyes Nervous system	Calm, Peace, Serenity, Connection to the Divine	Disconnected from the Divine, lack of Peace, Clarity and Focus
Third Eye	Indigo/violet	Between the Eyebrows	Eyes, Nose, Sinuses	Intuition, Clarity, Mindfulness, Creativity	Lack of Creativity and Clarity, Confusion
Throat	Blue	Throat	Esophagus, Trachea, Thyroid, Mouth and Throat	Communication, Self-expression, Truth, Openness	Unable to Voice Opinions, Judgement, Lies
Heart	Green	Heart	Heart, Lungs, Thymus, Circulation	Love, Connections, Healthy Boundaries, Empathy	Fear, No boundaries, Holding Back, Regret
Solar Plexus	Yellow	Belly Button	Stomach, Gallbladder, Pancreas, Spleen, Small Intestines, Liver	Stability, Connection Between Spirit and Body, Confidence, Emotional Center	Restlessness, Feeling Lost, Searching for Purpose, Strong Emotions
Sacral	Orange	Below Navel	Lower Spine, Large Intestines, Kidneys, Bladder, Reproductive Organs	Sexual Drive, Abundance, Physical Wellbeing	Critical, Self-degrading, Low Sexual Desire
Root	Red	Base of spine	Lower back, Colon, Legs, Hips	Stability, Groundedness, Security, Focus	Addictions, Anger, Fear, Resentment, Anxiety

Meditation to Clear the Chakras

Start with a few minutes of calm breathing to allow your body to relax and release. Close your eyes and visualize yourself in a beautiful meadow with lush green grass. Feel the grass beneath your feet as you walk through this meadow. Notice the flowers blooming all around you --- tulips, orchids, roses, whatever your imagination reveals to you. Listen for the sounds of any birds chirping in the distance. Feel a gentle breeze against your face and focus your attention on a beautiful willow tree in the distance. As you walk towards the tree, feel the warmth of the sun fill you with vibrant rays of light. When you reach the tree, imagine yourself sitting under the tree in a comfortable position with your back to the tree and its roots under your body. Sit back and imagine a brilliant red light flowing down from the sky, through the trees, into the crown of your head, and down to the base of your spine - to the Root chakra. Imagine the red light pouring into the fan of the chakra in a clockwise motion, illuminating and nourishing it with light and love. Allow the light to flow through your body and out through your toes. As the light gets absorbed by the Earth beneath you, it will wash away anything blocking you from living your full potential. It will release all that no longer serves your highest good, and fill you with strength and support. Now an orange light begins to flow down through the trees into your body and down to your Sacral chakra just below the naval, illuminating it with a vibrant orange light. Visualize the orange light entering in a clockwise motion through the fan of the chakra, allowing a burst of energy to flow through. This light fills you with abundance and emotional support as it penetrates every cell of your being. Allow the orange light to flow with ease, down through the body and into the ground beneath you. Next, a yellow light flows from the tree into the body and down to the Solar Plexus chakra near the belly button. Feel the bright yellow light as it connects your body and soul in peace and harmony, filling you with confidence and stability. Allow the yellow light to flow with ease and into the ground beneath you. Now a green light flows from above, through your head until it reaches your heart. Allow the light to fully penetrate your Heart chakra with an abundance of love, flowing freely through the fan in a clockwise motion. Accept this green light, as it represents all-encompassing love, and feel it penetrate every cell of your being. Next, a blue light flows freely down through your head to your Throat chakra, opening it up in a clockwise motion. This blue light represents your true voice, your ability to communicate with confidence; feel it flow with ease as it illuminates the chakra. A violet light now begins to flow through your Third Eye chakra in a clockwise motion, down through the body and out through the toes. The violet light strengthens your intuition as it flows with ease and penetrates every cell of your being. Lastly, a brilliant white light begins to flow down from the tree and through your Crown chakra just above your head. Allow this white light from the Divine to flow with ease, expanding and opening your crown to elevate your frequency. Allow yourself to become saturated in this white light for a few moments longer. When you are ready, open your eyes.

Connecting with Nature

Another way to balance the soul is to connect with the Earth. It is the part of our world that we often forget about. As we live our lives, from our home to the car, to school, to work and back home again, we get so focused on our routine that we forget to appreciate what our Earth has to offer. Its endless beauty is around us all the time, yet when we have our blinders on, we may miss it. Taking a walk in nature, sitting in a park on the grass, immersing yourself in the trees, the flowers and the natural air is soothing for the soul. When our bodies make contact with the Earth, it grounds us, soothes our vibrational frequency and balances our chakras. Spend 5-10 minutes a day enjoying the Earth's magnificence, whether it is the ocean, mountains, forests, lakes or simply a park. Take advantage of the endless supply of rejuvenating energy that Mother Earth has to offer us.

Grounding Meditation
If you can do this meditation barefoot on the grass, it will be more impactful. However, if that is not possible, you can do it in your home with your feet firmly on the floor.

Take a few progressive breaths to help relax your mind and body. Stand with your arms beside you, loose and limp, and both feet on the ground. You can close your eyes or keep them open if you are worried about losing your balance. Then simply ask Mother Earth if she can assist in grounding you, by rejuvenating you with the energy from the core of the Earth. Visualize the core of the Earth opening up as a brilliant white light cracking open like an egg. As the light pierces through, it travels up the layers of the Earth, through the ground beneath you and up through your body until it goes out through your head or Crown chakra. As the light travels through your body, it is revitalizing the body and soul, energizing and uplifting your vibration, grounding your body to the Earth's plane while connecting your soul to the divine as it exits through your Crown and travels up. Once the energy stops flowing (only a few minutes is necessary), thank Mother Earth for her bountiful gift.

Connecting with Animals

Animals are my favorite topic. As a Registered Veterinary Technician, I have spent almost 20 years caring for animals in a General Practice setting, Intensive Care and Surgical environments, and at the National Zoo. My passion for animals runs deep in my soul. I have a very real connection and respect for animals. As an only child, I grew up a little lonely, always wishing for a sibling while secretly loving the attention all to myself. It was through this longing for connection that I grew a deep connection with my first true pet, Chelsea, a German Shepherd. She became my best friend. I spoke to her, cried with her, played with her, trusted her and treasured her deep in my heart as the sister I didn't have. I still get emotional thinking about her memory and all she did for me as a child and a young adult. It was through that experience that I knew I wanted to work with animals in some capacity, to honor and cherish their instrumental part on the planet.

As an adult with pets that I now share with my children, I realize the magnitude of all that animals, especially pets, are here to do for us. They have a way of opening up our hearts in a way we didn't know we could. They have expansive and endless, unconditional love that pours out of them with no resistance or judgment. Domestic pets are one of the most positive influences in our lives, gifts from above that have come here to be our companions and our support system. There are a few differences between our most common household pets -dogs and cats.

Dogs really are man's best friend because they are here to be just that for us. They have no big life lessons to learn, no karma to release, no ulterior motives other than to be here for us. Generally, they are attached to one individual person in the house, but that is not always the case. They work with energy to absorb our energetic junk because they are able to process it and release it much easier than we can. Take notice the next time your dog jumps on you the second you walk in or puts its paw on you when you are on the couch. Dogs are not only doing this to get your attention, they are assessing your energetic flow and output. If they feel you are not able to release energetic junk on your own, they will happily do it for you. Everything is energy. If you go to work and have a confrontation with your boss and hold that negative energy inside and don't release it, it will become trapped inside your body. If too much of this trapped energy is stored in your body, then disease can occur. Your body always gives you subtle cues that something is wrong, but we often choose to ignore it, or we take a pill to temporarily mask it. Our dogs are master energetic investigators. When they recognize that your energetic state is unbalanced, they absorb it.

This ability stems from their energetic make-up, and their ability to use their 6 senses. They have an incredible ability to tap into their awareness and the world around them. They are in tune with the energy of the universe, subtle changes that most of us would never notice. When you walk in the door, they know immediately if you are happy, sad, frustrated or anxious. When you are in an angered state, they will stand at a distance and absorb your energy from a far, and when they sense you are calming down, they will get closer and closer. When you are sad and may be crying, they will attempt to touch you in some way, or lick your face. They are trying to communicate with you, send you love, and take on your pain. Dogs have this incredible ability to filter unwanted energy through their bodies with ease because they don't have the same thoughts that we do. Since they have no ego getting in their way, they just release. Since we tend to hold on to things in the form of energy, whether it is grief, frustration, anger, resentment or fear, we have difficulty releasing it because we simply don't know how or may not want to do so. Our dogs are happy to take that on for us as it flows from our bodies into theirs. They release it with no questions asked. So, when you see your furry friend again, give them a hug and thank them for being there for you, for taking on what you can't, for giving and loving you unconditionally, and for protecting you always.

Cats are a little different and are not always easy to figure out. They are the spiritual beacons brought here to protect us from energetic variations around us. They are not man's best friend because they come on a solo mission to keep their homes grounded and clear of negative energy. They sleep 75% of the day because they are connected to the Divine at all times and need to recharge their energetic batteries. While they do love us, they are less focused on trying to please us and more focused on their missions. They are too busy inspecting rooms of the house, chasing unwanted spirits away, and balancing our energy from a distance. They balance the home from top to bottom and from room to room. They are master energetic cleaners as they sweep the home and allow the good energy to remain. If you ever see them hissing at a corner of a room, or looking up at the ceiling while their head moves in half circles, these are the times they are busy at work, so try your best to let them be. When they do venture onto our laps, even for brief periods, give them thanks for their help with a gentle pet on the back. Just don't touch the wrong spot! If they are kneading you or purring, be aware that they are working with your energy too. Thank them for their mini treatment. If you are lucky enough to have a cat that is both loving and affectionate, be grateful and give them all the love in the world because they are truly special.

It is no wonder that animals not only lower our blood pressure, but also put a smile on our face and bring joy and laughter into our life. They are light-hearted and full of love and life. They are eager to be here with us, to support us, and walk beside us on our journey through life. They are incredibly healing for us. If you are blessed enough to have a pet, cherish and respect them for what they do for you every day.

For those of you who can't have pets, you can still benefit from their expanding love. You can volunteer at a local shelter and give back by helping them find homes. You can visit your local Zoo to sit and watch as the animals interact with each other. Just being in their presence is magical and uplifting. The simplest way to connect with animals is to go to the park, sit on a bench and watch as the local wildlife fly by you or run from tree to tree. Appreciate and enjoy yourself while you are immersed in their world for a few moments of your day.

Meditation to meet your Animal Totem

Everyone has an animal totem to assist them on their life journey. There can be one main animal and many others along the way to assist with different periods of transition. Animals are one of the easiest to connect with on a spirit level because they can lower their vibration to meet ours much easier than our guides. Animals are eager to communicate with us and are equally happy to work with us on the side lines, even if we are unaware of their presence on a conscious level. I have created an easy meditation for you to attempt to connect with one of your animal guides. Be patient if you don't see them the first time. They are there. You may need more time to see them. Keep trying as many times as it takes. Before you begin, surround yourself with protection. Ask that your animal meet you in the forest to reveal themselves to you and give you any messages they desire. If you see your animal, and it doesn't have a message for you, simply thank them for coming. Then take note of the first animal you see next. Don't second guess the animal that approaches. If you see a chipmunk and were secretly wishing for a panther, be grateful for what has shown itself to you. Each animal represents an aspect of our life that mirrors what we need the most. Look up the spiritual significance of the animals online or in an animal totem book to reveal the importance of their presence. It just may make perfect sense to you. The more frequently you do this meditation, the more you will notice that the animal changes based on what is going on in your life. If the same animal comes often, it is likely that it is your main animal guide who will be with you throughout your lifetime. The animals' messages to you may change each time. If you receive a feeling or a sensation, rather than a clear message with words, write all of it down. It will make sense once you put several messages together over a period of time. The important thing is to have fun with this meditation and not to get discouraged if you don't see anything initially. It may be that you need to work on balancing yourself first, and move to a higher floor on your High Rise before you can connect.

After a few minutes of progressive breathing, imagine yourself in a majestic forest with an abundance of trees and plant life. Visualize the ground beneath you - perhaps a path with rocks and small branches or lush green grass. Allow your imagination to be fluid and free. You hear a waterfall in the distance. Allow the sound to guide you. As you get close, the sounds of the water flowing over the rocks become tranquil music to your ears. As you approach the waterfall and the small body of water beneath it, you notice a small path that leads behind the waterfall. The path illuminates with an abundance of flowers on either side. Follow that path as it will lead you to your animal. Continue following the path until you reach a small, open meadow surrounded with trees. Watch until your animal comes to greet you in the small open area of grass. It may already be there or it may appear through the trees. Be patient and notice the very first animal that appears. Don't allow your conscious mind to interfere or second guess what you see. Once you have identified your animal, thank it for coming and ask if it has a message for you. Be patient and wait a few moments for thoughts to come through your mind or emotions to flow through. If there are no messages to be given, thank the animal for meeting you. Enjoy its presence for a few moments longer. Notice its body language and demeanor and how it may interact with you. It may brush up against you, stand beside you, or stare intently. Take note of what your animal does for its actions may contain a message intended for you. Once you are ready to leave, ask it if you can meet again another time. Watch as it disappears into the forest. Walk back through the pathway to the waterfall, taking one last deep breath, and open your eyes when you are ready.

Chapter 6
Re-boot: How to Shift into a New Perspective

Mindfulness

Living mindfully is elevating yourself to a new state of awareness. It's about shifting your perspective of life to the bigger picture as opposed to small fragments of time. When you look at a painting up close, you are drawn to areas of the picture that stand out to you individually, whether the color is stronger, the paint strokes are more vibrant, or your eyes are simply drawn in for no clear reason. We inadvertently divide the picture up, into what is comfortable for our eyes, and we may miss significant parts of the picture as a whole. Throughout our lives, we tend to compartmentalize our journey, whether it be childhood, college, career, relationships and family, and we break apart "our painting" into sections in the same way. By doing this, we may miss the greater opportunities. The bigger picture becomes weakened by limitations we set for ourselves. By taking a step back to view the full picture or painting of our lives, we would gain a better perspective on patterns we have developed, restrictions we have placed on our potential, and, more importantly, why they are there.

When we focus so much on the *now*, or dreaming only into the future, we ignore the past. This can be a self- protective strategy, as many of us have had traumatic pasts, or simply past memories we don't wish to revisit. This is completely understandable and a typical human approach to move forward and leave the past where it belongs - in the past. What we are missing in this strategy is that we are disregarding a vast majority of what makes "our painting" unique. We all have a story, good and bad memories, which shape who we become and who we continue to be in every moment of our lives. If we choose to close the door behind every milestone, we shut off that part of our self that can contribute to our collective Soul. All experiences are relative. The difficult ones shape us into better, stronger people. Good times bring us joy and remind us of how precious life can really be.

Living mindfully is imperative to our individual growth and collective growth as a society. If we live with clarity and open our eyes to the present moment while reflecting on the past, we can propel ourselves into the future in a more powerful and fulfilling way. In order to live mindfully, we must disconnect ourselves from the matrix --- the place that all people have been trained to operate --- and from the flow of societal norms dictated by traditions and centuries of beliefs. I believe that time is fluid. Our existence is ever-changing. The way we define our roles and the structure of our world must change along with it. What worked for the masses hundreds of years ago may not work for each of us, individually, in our modern world. We are different. We have evolved. We are on many different paths. No path is better than another. Each is unique in its own way. These paths and differences are not just defined by where we live, but also by what's in our hearts, and by what we feel, know and accept. When we are mindful, we are aware of not only ourselves, but also all those that are around us. We can see those that are doing great things, that are suffering, that are lost and afraid, and that are excelling and making a difference. We are aware and have compassion for everyone that is living out their human experience on their own path.

We have forgotten to live in the moment, to cherish the little things in life that make us smile and experience joy. We have forgotten how to disconnect and continue to play the game of life while not completely understanding what that means for everyone and how that may differ amongst cultures, sexes and societies. We know we must compete and strive to be the best. However, no matter how powerful we become and how much money we make, we realize that *winning* doesn't make us happy after all. The void we are trying to fill will always remain empty and unfulfilled if we don't re-evaluate and appreciate what truly matters. I always ask my clients if the shoes and material things that they have in life will be there for them when they need a shoulder to cry on or want advice on important life decisions. I ask them to evaluate whether all the *things* they are able to buy can take the place of family and friends. When they are asked to look at what is important to them with that perspective, they reflect and validate that, although money and success make things easier, they do not make them happy. This is not to say that many people don't find fulfillment or happiness from their career. It's simply about living for more than just that. It's about not limiting your "life painting" to one category.

If we expand our minds, the possibilities of what we can explore and create are endless. Living mindfully is about pulling back your sleeves, taking out all the colors in the bin, and creating your own unique "life painting" full of your own designs and brush strokes that fill and nourish your mind, body and soul, without limitations or worries of what others' paintings look like. Transforming is about living to *your* maximum potential. Each experience and choice you make stems from your own personal power and expand on one another to contribute to your ever-changing world.

Connecting to Your Own Place of Power

A large part of mindful living is connecting to the power within you. We all have endless capabilities. When we tap into the side of our self that stores our power, our true potential, we can manifest almost anything. Our power stems from a combination of all of our chakras, our Higher Self, and the Universal life force that is within and connects all living things. We all have access to this Universal network. You can think of it as the world wide web of our dimensional existence. Our connection to this network is much like wifi. It may be blocked, too slow or running at high speed. The higher we are on our emotional high rise, the more likely we are to have a better connection. Think about your high rise in relation to your chakras. The Third Eye and Crown chakras give you endless access to your Higher Self, your guides and the Universal Intelligence.

The lower levels correlate to the adverse effects of insufficient functioning lower chakras, causing fear, anxiety, and depression. When you are in the lower levels, your lower chakras will reflect and mirror those emotions, keeping you in a primal fight-or-flight state, significantly reducing your wifi connection, and blocking it all together. If you want to connect with your Higher Self, from where your personal power stems, you must first bring yourself to a balanced more mindful space. You must set an intention to live a life that is for your highest good and from your own inner truth. This will bring forth the empowerment and confidence to accomplish anything you desire. This can take some practice and adjustments. Once you allow yourself to follow a guidance system that comes from within, from your true source and not from social programming, you will not be misled.

To know whether you are receiving answers from your higher self, simply ask yourself three things before making any important decisions:

1. **Is this for my highest good and will it nourish my Soul in a positive way?**

   Take a moment to think about this. It is not a trick question, but rather a deep reflection of what is best for your soul and whether the choice you are making will project what it is that you want to put out into the world. For example, if you are trying to choose between two prospective job opportunities, one with slightly higher pay doing something that you won't particularly enjoy, and another lower paying job doing something you love, think about what will satisfy your soul as a whole. Try to ask yourself if the extra money is really worth it. You can find so much more joy in life when you fill your time with things that contribute to your life in a positive way.

   Many people are working day after day in a career they hate, and it is literally draining them of all purpose. They either lose interest in other things, or they try to overcompensate on their time off. This creates imbalance, more fatigue and pressure on themselves. This brings an endless cycle of disappointments and an overall dissatisfaction with life, causing depression and unhappiness. When you are faced with difficult choices, try not to reach your decision based upon your *wants*, but rather upon what the energetic consequences will be. If everything we say and do has energy attached to it, try to make your decision based on how you *feel* --- use your Intuition to guide you in the right direction.

99

2. Will this impact others in a negative way?

This is not to say that all of your decisions should be based on whether someone else will like it. Instead, determine if it will impact their life in an adverse way. Making decisions that benefit you, but put negative energy out into the Universe where it can harm others will allow the energy to find its way back to you. Nearly every decision that we make has a ripple effect, in your world, as well as upon those individuals who are connected to you in some way. Having empathy for others is a valuable attribute. If your choice can be weighed by considering what energy will follow, both positive and negative, it may help you tap into the part of yourself that knows the right thing to do.

3. Does this choice lead me closer to my vision and my purpose?

When we are forced to make an important decision, it is imperative to take the emotion out of it and determine whether the choice you are making will contribute to your life in a way that complements your goals. We certainly can't expect to fulfill all of our goals at once. They should overlap, much like steps leading to the next level of our metaphorical stairway to success. When making a choice, you can determine if it will lead you up a step or will cause you to backtrack. Sometimes in life we make the wrong choices, and we end up going down steps as opposed to continuously climbing up our staircase. It is important to be kind and patient with yourself when that happens. Refocus and proceed with clarity and intention. Reflecting upon your mistakes are opportunities to learn and develop a better connection with your Higher Self and strengthen your personal power and growth.

Meditation to Connect with Your Higher Self

After a few moments of progressive breathing, visualize yourself in a large meadow of lush green grass. Feel the warm summer breeze as it gently caresses your face. Look up into the sky at all the beautiful white fluffy clouds. Watch as one of the clouds descends from the sky and into the meadow, right at your feet. Allow yourself to get onto the cloud and lay back comfortably as this special cloud can hold your weight. Make the Intention to leave your conscious mind to rest in the safe space of the meadow below. Allow yourself to rise with the cloud back up in the sky --- slowly and freely, feel yourself rise. With every breath you exhale, you feel lighter and more relaxed. Just continue to allow the cloud to rise higher in the sky until you no longer can see the meadow below. As you continue to float higher, you reach a marble platform with columns on either side. Allow yourself to get off of the cloud and onto the platform. Visualize an Angel or Guide greeting you on this platform who will accompany you down the walkway to your Higher Self. As you continue down the walkway, you reach a special door that can appear any way you wish. This door leads to your own very special room where you can speak with your Higher Self, the part of you that stores the wisdom and knowledge of your Soul. When you are ready, open the door and allow your imagination to reveal to you what your unique room looks like. You will likely be greeted with a mirror image of yourself with slight variations. Imagine walking over and greeting this three-dimensional version of yourself, and pause to see if there are any messages, feelings or images that come to mind. Next, ask for guidance on a particular issue, and be patient while waiting for a response. It may come as flashes of images, words, thoughts or emotions, just let it flow without judgement. Lastly, imagine a beautiful pink light flowing back and forth between the two versions of yourself, from the base of the heart. This pink light represents self-love and care, allow it to flow with ease for a few moments as it rejuvenates your body and soul. Once you are ready to leave, return down the walkway until you reach your cloud, lay back down and visualize yourself descending back into the meadow. Once you get back on your feet, allow yourself to be grounded by remaining on the grass for a few seconds before opening your eyes.

Manifesting and Visualization

There are no words to describe the power of manifestation and its ability to change our reality. Consciously manifesting is putting out into the universe that which we desire. It can be for the little things in life, like getting an A on our history paper, making the basketball team, getting a shiny new car, or forlife changing events, such as getting that big promotion at work. Almost anything is within our reach, as long as it aligns with our highest good. In order to manifest, you must have a clear vision, as detailed and as clear as possible. If you have ever watched the genie in the bottle movie, you recall that no matter what the person wished for, they needed to be more specific in the details in order for them to get what they truly wanted. Don't give the Universe an opportunity to fill in the gaps. Be as specific as possible in your visions. Because our imagination is so vast, we can literally conjure up anything we desire. When we are young, our imagination is fluid and free. We can imagine whatever our heart desires with no hesitation. We can visualize ourselves on a purple unicorn, flying over a milky way of chocolate and ice cream, landing in a village of puppies and fairies, living in a house made of marshmallows where we had fluffy clouds as beds to sleep on, and endless games and fun. Children have no reservations. If they want something, they imagine themselves living their dreams with no blinders on. They go full steam ahead. They may not actually be able to manifest their dreamed reality. The point is that they are happy to try without holding back. For them, the sky's the limit. As we grow, we begin to put up walls based on experiences or lessons that shape our thoughts and reality. Our expectations shift from a dream state to more realistic expectations. The problem is that we often put so many limitations on our visions, from fear of failure that we overlook the possibilities we are offered. These possibilities can no longer be seen with the tunnel-vision we have created for ourselves.

When we visualize something that we want or an event to happen, we send out energy into the universe that matches the vibration of the emotions we feed into it. For example, if you are visualizing the game winning goal, you are feeling excitement, anticipation, and happiness at the prospect of it coming to fruition. Perhaps you are visualizing yourself running on the field, confidently making your way through the other team's attempts to stop you, visualizing yourself taking the game winning shot, and with ease the ball goes in the net! After making the game winning goal you are lifted up by your teammates as you all celebrate your team's victory. The energy attached to those emotions is transmuted through your vibrational field and out into the universe. Since those emotions are all high-vibrating, the energy will travel upwards, where it has the potential of manifesting with all the other positive energy that surrounds it. Consequently, if you have a fear, and you keep visualizing the potential of a negative experience in your mind, that can manifest as well.

The best example I can give has to do with what I tell all the expecting mothers who take my HypnoBirthing® classes. I explain to them that they have the power to dictate their birth experience. If they are immersed in fear and anxiety about their labor, and they allow that fear to replay in their mind repeatedly, whether it be previous birth traumas, pre-programming from movies depicting birth in a negative way, or underlining visuals that they create in their mind, these all have the ability to come to fruition. Not only are they showing their bodies over and over again how negative the experience will be, they are putting that energy out into the Universe to join with all the other lower-vibrating energies that cling to each other. This will create a field of negativity to follow them and ensures that their worst fear will come true because that is what they are manifesting into reality.

The saying, *"Be careful what you wish for,"* is very real, and people easily mistake visualizing their fears as innocent. What they don't realize is that every time they visualize the negative scenario, it becomes more real and validates the fear into a possibility. Don't give weight to your fears. Accept that you have them and think of the best-case scenario. The best-case visual may not always play out just like you see it in your mind. However, it is better than the worst-case scenario coming to fruition due to the continuous fearful attention and negative energy you send towards it.

Repetition is key

Once you have envisioned what it is that you are attempting to manifest, it is important to replay that vision as many times as you can. I recommend re-playing it in the morning when you wake up, following it by a positive affirmation such as, *"I will make a goal during Saturday's game,"* or, *"I will make a great executive once I get this promotion."* Combining an affirmation to your visualization will amplify the likelihood it will manifest.

Patience

Have patience because manifestation takes time. Once you send your wishes out into the universe, be patient as it may take some time for them to manifest. If there is a timeframe on your vision, such as the game taking place on Saturday, then it must manifest and take place during that day. However, if you are manifesting a car, it may take a while. Allow the energy to disperse into the atmosphere where the manifestation process can begin. Everything happens at the energetic level first. The physical manifestation will follow shortly after. Some people have visions of the future because they are tapping into the energetic manifestation before it becomes reality.

Detach yourself from the outcome

This is the most difficult part of manifestation. You really must be unattached to the outcome. That is easier said than done because you want the outcome to manifest according to your wishes and desires. It is important not to put too much weight on your vision. If what you are requesting doesn't align with your highest good, or the lessons you are here to learn, then they can't come to fruition. For example, you really want to win the lottery and you play every week, each time visualizing yourself winning, but you don't win. Try not to become discouraged. That just means it wasn't meant to be. Perhaps you signed up for a life where you have to learn the value of money and a windfall would not align with that theme. Again, only attempt to manifest goals which are attainable. If you don't get that promotion, it is likely that there is a better position lined up just around the corner. Don't lose sight of the intention. When you visualize yourself getting a new car, you must be open to the make and model. The Universe tries to answer our prayers. The results may not look like the original design in our head, but often times, it can be even better than we expected.

Section 3: Evolution

"Love is the bridge between You
and everything"
-Rumi

Chapter 7
Rejoice: Being the Best Version of Yourself

Throughout our evolutionary process as humans, there have been great advances and massive failures. If you look back at the overall history of mankind dating back thousands of years, human progress and setbacks seem to come in waves and cycles. The underlying themes that destroy our societies are greed, power, and wealth --- all stemmed from fear. Fear is the lowest-vibrating emotion. It sets the foundation for all other complementary emotions, such as anger, resentment, guilt, and worry. Once we have the ability to take back control of our emotional framework by tapping into our personal power, we can learn to control these emotions. By living mindfully, we catch ourselves falling down the levels of our high rise and quickly make the choice to go back up. It only takes a moment in time to change our vibration. If you just take one day for example, we can go through hundreds of emotions depending on what is happening throughout that day, riding up and down the elevator all day long. The important thing is that we end up somewhere on top by the end of the day. We are human. As humans, we have free will that is driven by our emotions. Our body is influenced by our mind. Our mind is influenced by our emotions. If we are emotionally balanced, we are motivated to accomplish our goals, which in turn makes us smarter, healthier and more driven.

There are many shifts currently happening in the world that affect us individually and collectively as we all play an important role in raising the vibration of the planet. The role you play and your transformation is vastly important for the collective New Earth transition. There are currently many exciting transitions of which we need to be aware. One of those is our children's evolution for they truly are our future. They say it takes one generation to make a change. While your elevation is valuable, the more players we have on our team, the more likely we are to evolve in a positive direction.

New Age Children

The state of humanity in the 21st century is alarming with the amount of hate, greed, and conflict steadily rising and leading to wars, mass shootings, genocide, religious persecution and discrimination. There have been large groups of volunteers coming to our rescue for centuries, incarnating as evolved souls, in an attempt to help us evolve. Unfortunately, due to the large amount of negative energy on the planet, it has become so dense and heavy that our rescuers have had a difficult time succeeding. At the turn of the 21st century, a large number of highly-evolved children came to Earth in large numbers to facilitate real change. As evolved souls, they would come in as babies and grow to be the next generation of compassionate, wise, and loving souls. These groups can be referred to as "*Crystal*", "*Star*" and "*Rainbow*" children. They all have unique personalities and capabilities that equip them to elevate the planet and to make a true shift in humanity. All of these children are special, unique, and powerful in their own way. I happen to be blessed with one of each of these children. Parenting them is challenging because they each process and react differently to most things. I have learned to get to know them as individuals, encouraging them in ways that complement their strengths and support them when they are faced with challenges that reflect their weaknesses. These New Age Children may overlap in age, and there may even be a few adults within their ranks. They signed up to be the first to come down with their skills to test the waters before the rest came. I will go into a brief description of the different types of children, so that, if you are a parent, you will be able to figure out which category your child resonates within.

Crystal

These children and young adults are between the ages of 10 and 20 today. This is just the typical range. They could be slightly younger or older. They are magnificent in that they are pioneers of the compassion movement. They are extremely loving and forgiving towards all people. They may not gravitate to any particular group of kids because they are friends with everyone. They become uncomfortable when there is conflict or an aggressive person present. Because their energetic make-up is so pure, they don't resonate with anger, judgement, or bullying. When they see war, shootings and discrimination in the media, they become turned off and unsettled because their soul doesn't recognize negativity towards one another. They are one of the first waves to follow the Indigos, which were sent here first, to remind us to love one another, to be kind to all types of people and all walks of life.

Crystal Children elevate you just by being in your presence. They have a beautiful light all around them and this reflects outwardly. When they look at others, they see the good in them. They are here to shift our perspective on humanity, to remind us to be good to one another because we all come from the same place. Although life is hard and dense, and at times unforgiving, we can still treat each other with respect and compassion. Crystal Children build bridges between people, expanding their love and light to anyone in their presence.
Because these children are so compassionate and caring, they possess a sensitivity like nothing we have seen before. They have even been labeled "Super Sensitive." Since they are so highly-vibrating themselves, they feel everyone's

energy, which makes them sensitive to shifts in vibrational frequency around them. They take empathy to an entirely new level, so much so that they care for others more than they do for themselves. They wish the best for everyone, which causes them to become overwhelmed at times. They may cry very easily, especially at the thought of disappointing others. If you are a parent of a Crystal Child, you probably haven't had to discipline them very often. They rarely misbehave because they want you to be happy. As their parent, you may also worry about whether they will be *eaten alive* in such a cruel world as they become adults. This is a valid concern, but they are here to take their blind love out into the shark tank, make friends with the sharks, perhaps inspire the sharks to be nicer to other sharks, and to spread their love and light to as many sharks as they can. They have a challenging journey, which is why only the wisest souls signed up for the job. They are easy going and filled with an abundance of love without boundaries.

Star
These children are typically 5 to 15 years old today, give or take a few years. These children were the next group to come, after the Crystals opened many hearts. Star Children swoop in with their charm, and start making changes. They are loving and compassionate like the previous group, yet they are armored with more of a backbone to assist them on their journey. Stars are the group of people who will initiate change in practically all facets of life. They are born leaders and will formulate the shift into how the world operates. They will be teachers, doctors, lawyers, officers, executives and entrepreneurs developing new and more Holistic methods to their area of expertise. Stars will pioneer these fields in a more compassionate, team building environment, to bring people together in a manner that will harvest a more cohesive and connected society. They are strong-willed, empathetic, steadfast and loving individuals who demand explanation

when told, "no." They are often wiser than those around them and they know it. Stars are the leaders of the future. They are here to serve as the anchors of society who represent genuine love and compassion. With their strong-willed nature, they will change the trajectory of our lives in one that is more mindful, respectful, and inclusive to all.

Rainbow
This group of children are currently being born and can be up to 6 years old. They are a unique blend of Indigo, Crystal, and Star Children. Rainbows are truly special, in that they utilize all the characteristics of their previous counterparts to make them transformational, high-vibrating superheroes, spearheading us into the future. They are compassionate, kind, sensitive, driven, stubborn and loving. They take leadership to a whole new level. They can be difficult to parent because they are competitive and ambitious from the moment they are born. When Rainbows crawl, they want to walk. When they walk, they want to run. When they run, Rainbows will sprint. Their endless energy will propel them to any finish line in life. Their combination of strong will, incredible drive, and empathy will supercharge their ability to do just about anything they desire. They will ensure that the new-world transition is a success, stopping at nothing to complete their mission. They will be widespread and work in just about any career, ensuring that they touch as many lives as possible. Rainbow children will bring people together. They will lift others up, stand by their side, and, even from a young age, they will bring change. They emit positive energy into the universe in large quantities because their goal is to elevate the planet with their light.

Divine
This group of children is the newest. There aren't many people that know about them. This will change very soon. Divines will be born during a brief window of time between 2019 and 2022.

I have been told by my Guides that they can only come through this brief opening because their energy is so expansive. They will have a collective consciousness with all the other Divine children, meaning they are directly connected to each other energetically. Individually, and as a group, they cannot be influenced by negative energy. They are an army of spiritually connected, powerful, evolved beings with no karma and no life-theme other than to assist the planet through its evolutionary transition. There is a lot more to say about these Divine Children, but, it will have to wait until I write another book.

Individually, all of these New Age Children are unique and special. Collectively, they will be a powerful unified army of evolved souls all playing their part, coming in waves of bright light to bring back positivity within ourselves and to bring solace and hope for our future generations.

Parenting These Children
Raising children in today's world can be intimidating and a heavy responsibility. Most parents are trying their best to find a balance between raising their children, work, and living their own lives. Prioritizing it all can feel overwhelming. When you add strong-willed and super-sensitive New Age Children to the mix, it can feel impossible to manage. Sometimes, the first child is easy going, adaptable and kind. Then, the second one comes out of left field and is stubborn, opinionated, and difficult. Parents are left feeling dumbfounded and possibly lost. The important thing to know and remember is that children are born with vast minds trapped in little bodies with minimal ways to communicate. Oftentimes, they are just looking for any way to get your attention. Children come into our lives to teach us to be more patient, empathetic and loving. They are little soldiers with a big job to do. Each person on this planet,

whether they are one day or one hundred years old, are evolved souls here to have a human experience. Much like animals, children tend to open our hearts in a way that we never knew was possible. They bring with them unconditional love and support, and are our biggest fans. Each child comes with a clean slate. It is how they are parented, influenced by family and friends and become experienced outside of the home that shape who they become. We are in a difficult time in our world, surrounded by so much negativity that we have, at times, lost hope. An abundance of these evolved souls have signed up to come here and help raise the planetary vibration by building bridges of love and compassion between all types of people. It is for this reason that these little humans are jam packed with knowledge and opinions. In their early years, it can be difficult for them to express these thoughts in an organized way. Sometimes, they need to unravel us and shake us to the core to prompt us to change our own ways and move out of our comfort zones.

Whether they are Crystal, Star, Rainbow or Divine, these children are equipped with a set of skills affecting all those who come into contact with them for a reason. The world needs the balance and comfort that these empathetic, kind, gentle souls provide. When we are at our lowest point, they make us believe in humanity again with the unconditional love that naturally emanates from them. They will become the leaders who take initiative, who are strong and confident, and who will inspire change for the benefit of all beings. New Age Children will implement these positive changes in ways which can really affect the vast majority of people.

Intuitive Parenting is about learning where your child lands on the spectrum by getting to know them intimately without judgment, and parenting them according to their needs, not yours. It is our responsibility to nurture and gently guide them in the direction that they are already headed with support, encouragement, and love. Unfortunately, many parents yell and shame their children for being disobedient at an age when the children really don't have the tools and maturity to express themselves. Children become frustrated because they feel that their opinions are not valued or accepted. They act out because that is the only way they can get the attention they are seeking. Parents often make the mistake of attempting to mold their child into what they want them to be and completely disregard their child's desires or provide little to no guidance. As a result, the child acts out, is not happy, and directs that frustration by underperforming in school because that is what they can control. This leads to a life of feeling unfulfilled, unsupported, and lost.

Once you have identified the characteristics and behaviors that make your child unique, take note that your child must be that way for a purpose. You may not know what this purpose yet. The important thing is to recognize that a purpose exists and to nurture them the best that you can. As a mother of three very different children, I have learned that they each have their own journeys. They have their own unique viewpoints and behavior traits that will complement them on their life's mission, whatever that may be. In the moments of arguments and breakdowns, try to think about how those experiences are molding and shaping our children for the future. It can be as simple as getting out of our own heads and thinking like a child to truly understand where they are coming from.

As an example, when I used to clean up my 4-year old's room, I would put all his toys in appropriate bins in a very organized way. He would come home from school and dump everything out onto the floor. I would react negatively and yell at him for making a mess. He responded to me once in a way that made me realize I was parenting from a place that was beneficial for me, not him. He said to me, *"When my toys are in the bins, I can't see them, so this way I know where everything is."* He didn't say it in an aggressive way. He was calm and explaining to me his point of view. While this helped me to understand his perspective and to see that his point is valid, I failed to provide him the opportunity to explain it to me before that moment. Afterwards, I re-organized his room in a way that he liked, including him in the process, making it easier to find his toys. We resolved that issue by moving forward in a positive way. He felt heard and respected, and I felt better knowing he wasn't just messing up his room to be difficult or to upset me.

Imagine being trapped in a little body with minimal ways to articulate what you want or need. With no real effective way to communicate, frustration overwhelms a child and crying and screaming are the result. Try getting down to a child's level. Sit down with them in a way that isn't so intimidating for them. Give children an opportunity to speak or show you what they are trying to say. Sometimes they just want to be heard, so that their point of view is considered and valued. If your answer to their request is ultimately "*no*," take a few moments to explain why and, even more important, tell them that you understand why they are upset. Give their feelings validation and recognize that you understand their resistance. Tell them that it is OK to be upset when we don't get what we want.

One of the most empowering things you can do for a strong-willed child is to give them choices. Knowing that they always have a choice makes them feel like they have more control, which is ultimately what they want. Instead of telling them what they have to do, try giving them choices that are within the confines of what is OK with you. For instance, instead of telling them they have to do a certain activity, give them several choices to choose from. You know that the options you are giving them are pre-approved by you, and your child feels like they are in control because they get to make the decision. Allow your child to be more involved in decision making, such as what you are planning to cook that week. Ask them for their input, schedule the meals out in advance, and there will be no surprises and no arguments. Children have endless amounts of energy and, just when you think they are spent, they pull out their reserves. If you say "no" to something they ask for and you cave in the tenth time they ask you, they have ultimately won. They don't take you seriously because they know at some point, they can break you. Be consistent, no matter how thin your patience is because I guarantee you will have to start over at ground zero every time they win.

Sometimes, in moments of anger and frustrations, we issue the most ridiculous punishments, like, "*No tablet for a month,*" or, "*I am taking this toy away forever.*" When you sentence your child to a punishment, make sure you intend to follow through with it. If you tell them, "No tablet for a week," and two days later, you fold and decide to give it back (most often for our own convenience), then all they learn is that their parents don't follow through. Try reprimanding them where it has the most impact, but for a shorter period of time. This way, they know you are serious, and they will learn to listen, so they don't lose their toy for another weekend. Children are often put in "*time out*" because they are deemed out of control. In reality, they are trying to burn off their endless supply of energy, especially in the winter months. To defuse a difficult situation when your child is burning off some steam, it may be helpful to excuse yourself for a "*mommy minute.*" Go into another room, take a breather, and come back to the room in a calmer state. It is normal for parents to get overwhelmed and tired, but often, children will feed off of their parents' emotions and mirror them. If you are tense and frustrated, your child will sense it, and even mimic your behavior. So, give yourself a time-out when you need it, and give yourself a break because you deserve it.

Super-sensitive children can be challenging in their own way. Because of their sensitivity, they can be perceived as weak. These children and young adults are not weak. They are little warriors of love that are here to teach us all how to open our hearts instead of closing them off. They are armored with endless supplies of forgiveness and genuine kind-heartedness. However, beneath this kindness is an underlying blockage when it comes to anger and negativity. They don't understand it, nor can they process it. Reacting to anger and to aggressive people is a New Age Child's biggest challenge. Because they vibrate at a higher frequency, they react differently than the average child to their angry parents or to mean children at school. They can't understand such anger and meanness because it doesn't exist in their world. It's as if they were dropped off in a foreign country where everyone around them was speaking in a different language, dressing differently, and acting abnormally. Their system goes into shock instead of fight-or-flight mode. Not knowing how to react, they freeze, cry, become sad, and break down.

The good news is that although they have to navigate through these challenges in a more mindful compassionate way, the rest of the world's people will learn from them. People will learn to change, to behave more like New Age Children, and to open their heart in a way that has laid dormant for years. We need more people in the world who operate from a place of empathy for all people they come into contact with. This is rarely a learned skill. It is a gift New Age Children are born with. There needs to be a balance between sheltering these children from negativity, so that they don't become overwhelmed, and supporting them to allow them to be themselves. These children can be taken advantage of easily due to their desire to make everyone happy. They may even put everyone else above themselves because they can't stand the thought of someone suffering.

If these children don't discover an outlet to release emotions, they will become overwhelmed. Meditation, mindful breathing, walking outdoors, cuddling an animal, journaling, and creative release by drawing or painting are all ways they can release energetic build up from toxic situations. "Toxic," for them, can be anything from watching a tv show where someone is harmed, witnessing bullying and shaming at school or, even worse, being bullied themselves. They may tend to keep their emotions inside out of fear of hurting someone else or making their parents worry. They need to feel trust and safety with their parents and know that they will not be judged and can speak freely. We were taught throughout childhood to not cry and hold emotions inside. Crying is an effective form of release, although throughout childhood we are taught not to cry, to toughen up. For boys, the message may come across stronger. We don't live in caves anymore. We don't live in times of fear when the man has to protect his family from attack by other tribes. It's time to stop telling boys they can't cry. This world is still a cruel and challenging environment. While boys and girls should be taught to be strong, in moments of anger, fear, and sadness, it is critical that they are taught that it's OK to feel and express their emotions.

Holding negative emotions inside is toxic and partly what is wrong with the world. Angry adults are walking the streets, holding their emotions inside ready to burst at the seams because they are afraid to release and be themselves. If we can teach our children, especially our sensitive children, that it is OK to cry and to release the emotions held within, they will grow up to be much happier and more compassionate adults.

In whatever shape or form it may take, allow them to be themselves. These New Age Children have their own ideas of what the world should look like because they are so open. Even if you don't necessarily like it, allow them to operate from a place of balance. Trust in them. Trust that they are strong AND sensitive. They have super powers unlike anything depicted in the movies. Allow them to do what they came here to do. Nourish them when they are young, and give them the unconditional love, security and freedom for each of them to grow into their own uniqueness. This will not only allow them to grow into early adulthood with confidence and empowerment, but will, more importantly, give them an appreciation and acceptance of themselves. As they mature to adulthood, they will look back and thank you for your willingness to grow along with them. Your trust in them will do more for them than any school could ever do. They will thrive. They will shine. They will spread their love to others.

Children can be intense, demanding and outright ungrateful at times. Parenting is a difficult journey full of rewarding and fulfilling moments, as well as times of desperation and tears. Strong-willed children seem to make any situation feel impossible. They test your patience every single day. They also unfold you in the most positive of ways and push you to be better. Today's children are forgiving and full of unconditional love and I believe that, at some level, they are aware of how difficult parenting can be. You are their rock, support, and guidance system. So, in the moments of pure panic when you feel like crying and giving up, look them in their eyes, tell them you love them and hug them tight. That may be all they really need. And it may be that you need it more than they do.

You Are Not for Everyone

All of us are unique in our own way. We evolve. We change. We shift. The people in our lives can either grow along side of us or veer off on another path. If we are living our true destiny, we make choices that are best for us at the time, and this may not resonate with some of the people in our life. We have to come to a point where we realize that we are not for everyone. That is OK. As children, we are vibrant and willing to think outside the box and to express ourselves with no reservation. We are beautiful and confident little bodies with no fear. Unfortunately, as we grow, we are told to live within the confines of traditional societal norms. Our parents begin to shape us into what they want or think we should be. Other children at school bully us if we stray outside of what's comfortable for them. We are made fun of. We are ridiculed until our creative life source is beaten out of us. We then become shells of ourselves, and grow up feeling lost and confused.

It is no surprise that so many adults cannot find their true selves, that part which is vibrant, unconditionally happy, and of light. If we could change our mind-set, and teach our children to accept themselves and others for who they are --- encouraging them so they can continue to grow and mature like a beautiful flower, they wouldn't wilt away and become part of the soil like the mass majority. We must empower our children to be unique, to be the star they want to be. If everyone lived by that intention, we would all grow up happier and healthier adults.

In order to truly evolve, we must ensure that we are operating from a place of balance and creative expression, which of course is what separates us from one another. Other people will either like the energy you put out and find pleasure being in your presence or they won't. It's about accepting the fact that you are unique, you can't make everyone like you. This would be an impossible task that would drain you of your true essence should you choose to embark upon it. Do not mold yourself into what others want you to be. Strive towards accepting and loving yourself the way that you are. It is from that place that true peace will follow. As you walk in your true path, fully vibrant and in a state of complete self-acceptance, those who match your frequency and align with what you represent and stand for will come into your life for the right reasons and at the right time. Those people will be your beacon of support to help gravitate you towards the direction you are already headed. They will ground you and lift you up when you need it. You will do the same for them. Cherish yourself. Accept and love who you are. Allow those who don't appreciate you to continue on until they find their match, their group which will be the right fit.

Chapter 8
Elevating Your Mind, Body and Spirit

Through the process of transformational healing and evolving to the best version of ourselves, we will find immense peace and gratitude for life. It wasn't until I was deep into my own spiritual journey to find my purpose, figure out why I am here, and how I could help in some way that I realized I was overthinking it. I feel as though I am not alone in this regard. Many of my clients ask that exact question - *"What is my purpose?" We put so much pressure on ourselves as if we feel this intense pressure to* figure out this missing puzzle piece and place so much significance on it that it ends up consuming us. Many spend countless moments of our life soul-searching, praying, traveling, and reflecting with the hope that we will discover this deep revelation we are striving for. Instead, we end up finding ourselves unfulfilled and lost because of all the striving.

It wasn't until I was lost, unsatisfied and frustrated with myself that I shifted my focus to self-care, meditation, and simply enjoying my life, my husband, and my children. I decided to focus on being a better person and a good role model for my children, and vowed to help those who come into my center to the best of my ability. It was through this transition and a process of letting go of expectations, living in a way that I was comfortable, and not caring what anyone else thought, that allowed the layers of myself that I didn't like to surface. I focused on truly loving and accepting what was left: a raw version of *Sherri.* I began to feel more at peace and more translucent. I came to realize that we all have the same purpose, and it is simple. There is not one person better than another. It is how we choose to serve that defines our uniqueness. We are all here to learn and grow, of course. It is through the learning process that we understand how to be with others and ourselves in our darkest and weakest times, and how to show gratitude and compassion for others as they too are growing and evolving at their own pace, on their own path. It is how we treat others that will determine our purpose. Whether it is as a doctor of medicine, a teacher of the young, a free spirit that wanders the planet or a high-level executive, it is irrelevant how we choose to spend our time here. What matters is how we choose to treat others. We must operate from a place of humility and grace towards all beings in the way we behave towards others while competing for the same job, in the way we tend to sick patients, in the way teachers influence their students, and in the way we function as a society.

If you are ready to elevate your mind, body and soul, you must be ready to expand your awareness beyond your comfort zone by living more freely, appreciating the little things, and being more grateful for what we have versus striving for what we don't necessarily need. You will find your purpose when you stop looking for it. It's about awakening our minds and tapping into our higher self, so we can be guided with clarity and awareness about what is actually happening on this planet. We desperately need to be elevated out of this dense, negative, and debilitating energetic state of our current world. People are waking up all over the world. With conviction and honesty, they take their blinders off and step out of the assembly line that the large mass of humanity follows. We are led to believe that our world needs to operate in a specific way. Depending on where we live, we are guided by many leaders who are drowning in their own negativity and relentless thirst for power to feed their own rapacity versus looking out for the highest good of their people. We are being influenced by the negative energy in our atmosphere that is spreading like wildfire and blinding us from our truth. We are so hypnotized that we have lost touch with reality. We are in desperate need of positivity and light to overcome the darkness, and every person counts. If you are trying to figure out your purpose, start by opening your eyes. Spread your positivity and light to elevate the vibration of the planet for future generations.

Everyone Has Their Line

Whether it was lining up for recess or going to lunch, you may remember your time in grade school when you had to stand in lines for just about anything. Standing in lines was a large part of growing up, as well, waiting your turn to get to the next thing. It was through my journey that I discovered that everyone also has an energetic line. Everyone has an energetic line of people behind them that represent the number of people they will help at some point in their life. I believe we all come to this Earth with the ability to make an impact in someone's life or to help them in some way. Some people will have a short line behind them. Others' lines will go on for infinity depending on how far they can spread their light. To explain this a little better, I will take you back to a meditation I did early on in my spiritual journey. My grandmother had passed away years prior, and she often came to me with messages and guidance when I needed it. It was during one meditation that she showed me sitting at a table with a woman I didn't know. I was face to face with this person and knew I was helping her in some way. I just didn't know how at the time. The vision expanded to where I could see someone standing behind her. I assumed it was the woman's friend, but when I looked beyond her, I saw another person, and another until the line just kept going as far as I could see. I told my grandmother I didn't understand what that meant, and she explained that she was showing me *"My Line."* I was thinking, "what they could possibly be standing there for?" and, "how I could help them?" Since this was so early in my journey, I had no idea what to do with my gifts because I was still discovering them. She told me not to worry about the details and that I needed to understand that those were the people whom I am meant to help in my life. They were lining up energetically for when I was ready. She said they wouldn't all come at once, and I had already helped some without even realizing it. As I matured and opened my awareness, they would come in a steady flow. It was such an amazing vision and a little overwhelming. I didn't know how I would help them at that point in my journey; yet, the anticipation and excitement filled me with the motivation to find out. Now, many years later, with a steadily flowing line as far as I can see, I remain humble and grateful to help each and every one of them.

Let me explain more about how this Line works. I believe that every person has a Line. The length of Line will vary, and Lines can certainly overlap. For instance, I have a Line behind me, but I am also in the Lines of another, as I need help as well. Whether the Lines I have been in were behind my teachers, mentors, physicians or friends, they helped elevate me in some way. The people in your Line can be on your path for a brief moment when you happen to be in the right place at the right time to assist them, or they can come in your life for you to help them in a much more impactful way. The more empathetic and willing you are to serve others, and to brighten them with your love and light, the longer your Line will be. If everyone in the world was aware of their Line and open to the idea of helping others, they would gain more satisfaction from life. They would find more purpose, and see others in a different way. There would be no greed or hate. There would only be compassion. One of the easiest ways to live your life is to treat others how you would want to be treated. This is something I try to instill in my children every chance I get. It is such a simple premise, yet many people walk around oblivious to others they don't know, as if they are simply "paid extras" in a movie in which they are the star. It is simple to change the theme of "your movie." It just takes an Intention to treat everyone as equally important as the main character. If you find yourself judging someone, just think to yourself, *"could that person be in my Line?"* Even if they are not, they are in someone else's Line, so try to give them a break.

Building Bridges

Once we change our awareness and open our hearts, we can expand our beacon of light to touch as many souls as we can. One way we can do this is by building bridges of energy to create a more harmonic world to live in. Think about the Universal intelligence that connects all of us on an electromagnetic level. It is a place where our higher states of consciousness recognize that we are all one. Imagine what would happen if we brought that into our physical reality. We could manifest energetic connections at a deeper more personal level. If we create societies in which we build bridges bringing people together, as opposed to walls to separate them and create hierarchies that lead to discrimination and abuse of power, we can reverse a lot of the damage that has been done. This has to happen on a personal level where each and every person opens their eyes to live more collaboratively and mindfully. If we can build small bridges of our own, branching out to people, we can create a network much like a hundred-year-old oak tree with its mighty branches extending outward, intricately connecting from one solid foundation, and growing with love and integrity. It starts with gestures and small branches. Others will begin to follow. They will build upon each other and connect in miraculous ways. When you are looking to evolve your soul, once it has been nurtured and loved, think about ways you can help others build their bridges.

Our societies are created on a foundation of hierarchies and controlled levels of power. When we cultivate environments of teams, a collaborative partnership can naturally exist to realize common end goals. This may be a near impossible concept for older generations to grasp. Given the societal structures and norms in place, it is no surprise that young adults who embark into the workforce feel insecure and uninspired. There are no jobs or careers that motivate them from a soul level. That is why so many young adults are becoming entrepreneurs. They are putting their future and desires in their own hands. Generation Z's, or however we want to refer to them, are hitting a wall as they become legal adults and are forced to go out into the working world. I see many of these teens and young adults who come to me feeling lost and confused. They don't agree with the way companies are being run, and they don't know what to do with their lives. I explain to them that this is for a good reason because they are the generation of change. They are the ones that will say, *"Enough is enough!"* and will literally re-shape our future. They are strong, resilient and have the benevolence and drive to pull it off. They just need more people to encourage them to spread their wings. Most of them are being raised by parents with old ways of thinking that they must live their lives in a specific way because that is what the parents were taught and are comfortable with.

These parents don't know how to support their children as they grow up and are turned off by the way society operates. This new generation can feel this in their soul. They know something is not right. They are tapping into the Universal Intelligence that encourages them to bring out the child in them, to be different and start ventures that will involve, support, and all involved to grow.

Chapter 9
Elevating Others

Once we build bridges to bring people together, we can take it one step further by elevating the vibrations of others to match our own. Since energy is attracted to that which resonates with its vibration, it can either assist in the elevation of the energy around it, or gravitate away. Gravitating away from one another is how we are currently living in this world, like we are all little drops of oil in a large body of water. We spread out, trying not to touch anyone around us. It is like the walls we have built around ourselves for protection block us from experiencing connections. Once we break down the barriers that separate us, we can elevate from our physical self and see others as souls of light. If we all expand our light as far out as possible, whether that be through helping one person at a time or large groups (school teachers, public speakers, authors, etc....), change will follow. It's about taking the initiative and following through on your Intentions.

Our bodies are absolutely incredible systems of self-healing. We need to take a moment to think about how our bodies work tirelessly to keep us at homeostasis despite environmental factors. Our autonomic nervous system is working every moment of our lives to ensure we are balanced or protected in dangerous situations. Our heart pumps with the harmony of our body nurturing every cell with oxygen. When we are injured, our bodies work diligently to heal our wounds. Our bodies can heal our bones when they break and mend our skin back together when it tears. Since our bodies provide a seemingly unlimited source of self-healing, the question becomes, "Why do we set limitations on what else it can do?" Our body and soul gracefully operate together, flowing with the waves of energy in the atmosphere, aligning with the electromagnetic field that surrounds us, and tapping into the Universal Life force to sustain us. Many of us rely so heavily on western medicine and pharmaceuticals that we have become disconnected from our bodies. It is as if we have lost faith in our body's ability to Heal more than just our superficial wounds. Our mind is so powerful that if we set no limitations on what our body can do, it will follow our lead. Restoring faith in our body starts with our emotional health, it is the gateway to balancing our soul. We must invest ample time and energy in our emotional well-being, as much as we would for anything else, if not more.

We are making strides to demystify our differences by wiping away labels that once separated us - one human from another. By creating a society where every person is created equal, we can begin to heal the wounds of not only our souls collectively, but also those of the Earth - our home. There are many examples that show the progress being made, starting with gender equality. I have been shown a time in our future where our gender will not define who we are or what we can become. The future generations will look back at the previous centuries in their history books with confusion and disdain as gender roles will be a foreign concept. We are moving to a time where our roles will shift, where the roles of men and women will overlap to become more symmetrical, where neither gender will be superior to the other. We have seen this transition through many pathways, one being homosexuality, as we are coming to a period when this can finally be accepted as part of society. This has led to gender neutrality where a whole generation of people prefer to be accepted by what they can contribute versus identified by their physicality. Some evolving new parents are raising their own children as gender neutral, so they can one day decide for themselves how they want to be identified. We are still in the early stages. Older generations are having a difficult time grasping this concept. Nonetheless, they must try to open their mind soon. This will continue to manifest whether they are on board or not. We have seen this with the *MeToo* movement as well, where masses of women have had enough of gender discrimination and sexual abuse, and will no longer tolerate it. Equal pay for genders has made much progress, to the point which many males are standing up for their female counterparts to ensure they are paid the same.

As we continue to evolve, similar shifts will accelerate the momentum as we transform our societies to be more open, relaxed, and accepting. The meaning of life is not as mystical as the unicorn. It is simple, uncomplicated and accessible to all of mankind. If we treat others as we want to be treated and open our hearts, we can assist in elevating the planet through Transformational Healing. We can guide and support others with patience and kindness, remembering that our souls are wise and all loving. It is when we identify too much with our physical bodies that the density of the atmosphere will cloud our ability to see clearly. The excess of negativity around us can influence and tempt us to divide our soul and body as if they are two different entities. Once we decide to reconnect the mind, body and soul, we can awaken our spirit to the endless possibilities within our reach. If we all expand our light, we can dissolve the darkness. Love will travel through all outlets of humanity, like a wildfire of Divine light until it reaches all depths of this Earth. Only then will we be free to expand and build upon a foundation of Peace and Joy. Only then can we provide a bright future for future generations. Call upon your inner strength to operate from *your truth.* It is from this place of truth that a ripple effect of positive energy can freely flow out to all of humanity.

Meditation to connect to the Universal Intelligence

After a few minutes of progressive breathing, visualize yourself in a tunnel of light. Begin walking through the tunnel. The farther you travel through it, the lighter you feel. The tunnel is both relaxing and calming to your mind. As your vibration continues to rise, allow yourself to release the baggage of emotions you are carrying. With each breath and with every step you take, shed the lower vibrational energy that has been following you and holding you back. Now that you are connected with the rhythms of your Higher Self, you are ready to connect. Imagine that this tunnel begins to dissolve into the light it is made of, creating a beautiful prism of colors. As the tunnel transforms itself, visualize flashes of red, orange, yellow, indigo, pink and violet. As you allow each one of these colors to flow through your entire being, all your energetic layers begin to vibrate in an expansive manner. Feelings of euphoria wash through your body as your frequency steadily rises to meet the Universal Consciousness. A tunnel of energy opens above your body, A vortex of warm and welcoming energy envelopes you as you are pulled through it. A powerful yet gentle energy vibrates through your body, expanding your ability to connect to the Oneness of the Universe. In that moment, ask to be connected to the Divine, to the Universal Intelligence which connects all of mankind. Ask for guidance and anything you need to be shown at that time. Wait patiently for thoughts to begin pouring through your mind, for visions to appear, or for emotions to unfold. Allow yourself to stay in this space as long as you need until you feel ready to connect back with your body. When you are ready, visualize yourself back in the tunnel of light and walk through it. As your body and mind slowly integrate, you may feel heaviness or tingling throughout your body. Ask the universe to help ground you and bring you back to the present moment, feeling refreshed and energized. Open your eyes when you are ready. Allow yourself to slowly acclimate back to the room. Do not attempt to stand up too quickly. Remember to write down in your journal what you experienced.

Messages from Spirit

Spirit has a beautiful gift for all of you. A group of Spirit Guides, Archangels and Ascended Masters leave you with their own unique messages for those willing to listen to their gentle guidance.

Chala- My Spirit Guide

"We wish to communicate with the masses of people who are willing to expand upon their visions with willingness to operate from a place of truth, a place where their souls can expand with the flow of the universe, where love flows like running water into the sea, with the gentle caress of the universe as we try to guide each one of you in the right direction. Do not despair, for at this time the density is both blinding and powerful. As your bodies are having difficulty walking amongst the negativity, it feels as though you are walking through quicksand as it takes hold of you, taking you down with it, while your soul yearns to be free. Your soul calls upon the Angelic Masters of the Divine to rescue it from this place, as if life is too difficult. You call out and wish to be rescued, as the burden of this life and this negativity is too expansive. You are drowning in it. You call upon us to remove you from this negative period. We ask that you use this opportunity for growth as you band together with your brothers and sisters to create the environment with which you desire. You don't understand that you are in control. Yes, you are in control of this universe: which direction you gravitate towards is what will pull you, a force both strong and destructive if you allow it to be. The mind is such a fragile thing. It can be influenced by the wind as it blows in different directions, taking you along with it. So vulnerable is the human mind. It is such a conflict since the soul is strong. It is interconnected with the One, the Universe, the Divine and is so much more powerful than the mind, yet

you allow the mind to control you. "Why do you do this?' we ask. If you pull from the Universal intelligence, you can no longer be fooled by the darkness. The negativity on Earth will dissolve into your light because the light of the Divine Consciousness is more powerful than anything else in your world. We invite you to open up that side of yourself, so that you can live in harmony. We do not wish to see you suffer, as you have free will. We also can't interfere with your choices, or how you live your lives. We ask that you free yourself from the darkness by simply choosing the light. The brighter you shine, the higher your vibration will be. This is what the negative forces rely upon: your weakness to succumb to the lower vibrations, making the world heavy, filled with worry, disease, sorrow and fear. Those are the most powerful emotions, and they conflict with the highest vibrations of love, peace and joy. We all have the right to live in harmony. Having a human experience without the violence and pain is not what you are sent down to learn. You are sent down to work together and to have compassion and kindness for your brothers and sisters. We all come from the same light. Because souls come down in their earthly flesh, they forget where they come from, what they are here to do, and how to evolve. That is due to the limitations that you set for yourself and is influenced by the negative environment around you. Remove yourself from the darkness and into the light. You will see with clarity, honesty, and truth. We ask that you expand your hearts to allow others into your space, into your life, to help one another through this dark time that you find yourselves in. We ask that you assist the children as they grow and prepare the Earth for a brighter future for all. Nurture them and watch them grow and blossom into beautiful bouquets of grace as they elevate this planet, so we can continue to live in an abundance of love. Love is the answer. If we love, there will be no hate. Why do you allow hate to fill your heart? The heart needs to flourish. It must feel free. It must expand its beauty to all living souls on this Earth. This planet is your home and She welcomes you with open arms. Don't punish Her for that love. She is hurting from your lack of compassion for the home She provides you. She calls upon you to heal Her wounds. She is suffocating in your ignorance as a mind driven human being. She knows better of you. She feels each and every one of your souls. She feeds off the light that you carry, and understands the density that has become her reality, as she must hold the space for us all. She can't hold the space much longer. She is in desperate need of healing. It starts with you healing yourself, so that you can heal Her through your expansiveness. The brighter your light shines, She will heal Her wounds. She will greet you with gratitude, and through that healing will come love for all that walk the Earth."

Archangel Raphael

"You are in desperate need of healing. Your bodies are weakened by the negativity on Earth. Your bodies are struggling to operate in a balanced manner. I encourage you, my light-workers, to invest your time and energy into yourself, into your body as this is the vessel you have chosen to assist you in this life. If you do not respect it --- by working too many hours, by feeding it food that is lacking the energy that you need, by sleeping less so that you can accomplish more with your time --- you will parish before your time. For what I ask of you is, 'What is really important?' 'Is the job you have chosen so important that you are willing to sacrifice the body that fuels you?' I ask that you prioritize your body first, so that you can do all that you desire in this life. You cannot help others if you are depleted. If your energetic tank is lacking, you simply can't thrive when your body is aching for love. Pour love into your body with the food you eat, the emotions that you feel, and the people that you surround yourself with. All of those things matter equally, as they are all important to align you energetically, leading to a more balanced body and soul.

Your soul Is expansive and connects to the Divine every moment of your existence. It is your lifeline to your body that continues to formulate the energy for your heart to continue beating the Universal Life Force, as you tap into every moment, as all beings are connected and can nourish themselves from this source. Do not limit yourself and your capabilities by disrespecting the vessel that carries your soul. Our bodies are designed to be strong and durable. It is love that drives the body and soul together. Nourish this soul with the fuel of manifestation by mindfully eating and carrying on in life doing things that really make your spirit light up with joy. That is what life is all about. You are encouraged to enjoy every aspect that life has to offer you. Yes, you have lessons to learn, and work to do, but this does not limit the joy and the capabilities of happiness and enjoyment on your journey to greatness. We walk with you, beside you and behind you, protecting you, healing and supporting you as much as you request of us. There is no limit to your abilities, as manifestation is endless. Heal your body. Heal your soul. Heal your spirit. Heal all. Your light and love are powerful enough to lift you up when you fall, to guide you through the darkest moments, and to elevate you from the most challenging times. Call upon us to guide you as you need us. We will be there, ready and willing to serve you. We believe in your power. We ask that you, too, believe in yourself. Your bodies are greatly controlled by your mind. It is the driving force in your life. Do not let this mind take hold of you. It is not meant to control you. It is meant to assist you when needed. Tap into your Higher Self. That is the true source. You will not be misguided. Give your body credit. It's possibilities of healing are expansive, limited only by your beliefs. Remember this when you are at the end of your road, with no more physicians to see, no more medications to try. Look at yourself in the mirror and ask if you are ready to heal, if you are ready to trust in yourself again, to move forward with courage, with clarity and composure. We believe in each and every one of you --- 'Do you believe in yourself?'"

Archangel Gabriel

"Divine beings, I call upon all of you, as we are all of the Divine source. The center of all of our souls are connected, as our light permeates through all beings on Earth as well as other planets --- furthermore, through all Universes. You are all connected, and we ask of you to consider this of all the people in your life, those you encounter and even those you will never meet. You are all of the Divine, the center of creation, all light-workers. We urge you to call upon your souls to guide you. Many of you have forgotten your purpose and are drowning in your own Free Will. That which was granted to you as a gift has proved to be your biggest challenge. 'Have you been given too much freedom?' is a question we ponder. As generation after generation is born and succumb to the negativity, which only grows stronger with time, not weaker. I speak to you with urgency as you are at a time that demands that you open your eyes, at once, before it is too late. We beg of you with the utmost stern, yet gentle voice, as we fear you do not understand your future if you keep living this way. The solution is simple, yet many of you don't believe. Love seems too easy an answer. 'If that notion is so easy, why does it challenge you so?' 'Why is it so difficult for you to look at your neighbor with loving eyes, the same as you would for your child?' You all come from the same place, and return together. It is your time here on Earth that burdens you. The density and darkness on Earth alters this Free Will. It tempts even the strongest, praying on the weak and targeting the brightest light, as it is blinding for the Dark Beings. They wish to dim your light until there is nothing left, but a body without a soul to fill it. It is the soul that fuels the body with love, and with that love, raises your vibration. Look up to the sky, Will yourself to elevate out of the darkness. It is your choice. It is that simple. We give promise to you that we will not turn our backs on you as many of you

have on us. We have endless love and compassion for every living being on Earth. All life forms have the capacity to produce positive energy, which can withstand any form of evil --- so long as you believe in the light. Walk in the light. Don't turn back. Trust in your children as they will guide you into the future. There are better days ahead if you all work together hand in hand and trust in one another. Remove yourself from the cement you have put your feet in. Walk freely with an open mind and an open heart. Cherish this life, your body and this Earth. Treat everyone as you would treat a beautiful flower blooming in the Spring warmth. Nourish the soil it thrives in. Expand the warmth it radiates in. Water it delicately and saturate it with kindness. Take a deep breath. It's not too late. Put out your hand to help others. Be the light. Feel the light. Own the light. Send an abundance of love to all."

Archangel Metatron

"I would like to address with you Free Will. This is what makes your Earth unique. There are no other galaxies where the beings that inhabit other planets have Free Will. This was intended to be a gift for humans on Earth. You are sent down to Earth as a soul that merges with a body, to become One. The memories of past lives and Spirit are covered with a veil the moment you are born, so that you can fully immerse yourself in the human experience. Yes, you have chosen your life purpose ahead of time, and those who will be in your life to assist you. However, you are given Free Will to make choices which align with that purpose. When your Free Will becomes vulnerable to lower energies, you are tempted, which leads to a life of dead end paths. When you walk in the dark, there are no paths to enlightenment. There is only despair and darkness. Those that are weak because they have lost love for themselves lower their vibration. They attract other lower vibrating souls to surround them and create a vortex of negativity. If only you can see the world from our viewpoint, you would understand that the same Free Will that brought you to the darkness can also bring you to the Light. It only takes a moment in time. Time is a relative term because we have no time here. The Universe is all connected in many timeframes. As they all connect, many realities exist at once. Even on Earth, there are many realities being played out. Only you can't see them at your limited vibration. Do not let your Free Will captivate and take hold of you. We plead with you to use your Higher Consciousness to direct you in the right path. Use your Free Will for the pleasures in life --- which movie to see, which delicacy to choose that nourishes your body, and which country to visit. All the choices that bring joy to your life is what your Free Will is designed to do. Humans are unique and all very different. Although connected with the Universe, we ask

that you explore what makes you different. Shine in your own light as that will make you thrive. Free Will is a gift to surround you with many choices that align with what makes you special, to feed your spirit with an abundance of experiences. We ask that you walk forward in your power, in control of your path, and not bound like a puppet while you follow the lead of others. You are brighter than that my children. I send my light in hopes that it finds its way to your soul, permeating through all that you aspire to be, to elevate all of humanity. I stand with you to protect, to restore and to hold all of you in my hands. Fly free like birds. Allow the wind to gently guide you. Let go and trust in your knowing that all is as it should be."

Archangel Ariel

"For the beautiful souls reading this book, I would like to discuss Karma. Many live by the notion, "What you put out comes back to you." Although this is true, you are in a period where the Karmic wheel will not stop spinning as long as humans keep making the same mistakes. We understand the temptations and the emotions that drive you. After centuries of time, humanity is still chasing its karmic debt. It is time to wipe the slate clean and move forward with clarity and peace, for your past sins will no longer weigh you down. They will no longer control your existence, determine your successes, nor block your happiness. Change needs to occur. We encourage you to move forward with a clean slate and a positive outlook. We ask that you treat others with kindness, so you can elevate the planet with your expanding light, and not weigh it down with your emotional baggage. "Let it go," we ask. In fact, we say that you have no choice. You must let go of all that no longer serves you at this time in order to move forward. There are alternate realities for which you are striving --- an existence of emotional freedom filled with desires, which encompass all living beings. This is a possible reality that is within your grasp if this is what you choose. Your reality is what you make of it. Call upon the Archangels to guide you, and open the door to everlasting abundance. We are happy to provide pillars of support. We hold no judgment on your weakness, as we understand your struggle. We send endless love and light to all who are willing to accept it."

Made in the USA
Las Vegas, NV
16 December 2022

63045583R00085